NECROMUNDA®

HOW WONDROUS IS NECROMUNDA, A WORLD THAT FEEDS UPON ITSELF LIKE ANCIENT OUROBOROS EATING ITS OWN TAIL.

WITHIN THEIR COCOONS OF PLASTEEL AND CERAMITE, MEN LIVE AND DIE UPON A DIET OF TOIL, VIOLENCE AND MISERY. THEIR SWEAT FALLS TO FORM THE RIVERS FROM WHICH THEY DRINK, WHILE THEIR FLESH BECOMES A MEAL FOR THEIR DESCENDANTS; NOURISHING A GENERATION UPON THE REMAINS OF THE ONE BEFORE. LIKE THE MAGGOT THAT BURROWS INTO THE MEAT OF A CARCASS, THEY THRIVE AMONG THE DECAY, STRIPPING THE ROT AND SPOILAGE FROM THEIR HOMES AND PILING UP THEIR KIN WITHOUT THOUGHT OF RITUAL OR REMORSE. WITHOUT THE DEAD, THERE CAN BE NO LIFE. EACH HIVE CITY IS BUT A CHARNEL HOUSE WHERE BILLIONS ENDLESSLY LABOUR, UNAWARE THAT LITTLE SEPARATES THEM FROM THE CRUMBLING WORLD THEY SCAVENGE TO KEEP THEMSELVES ALIVE.

ONLY THE GANGS COMPREHEND THEIR EXISTENCE, FIGHTING AND KILLING, BECAUSE AFTER ALL – WHAT VALUE HAS LIFE WHEN YOU ARE ALREADY DEAD?

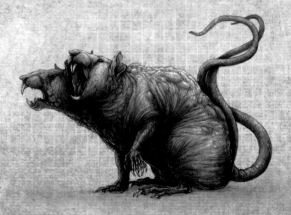

CONTENTS

2

Printed in China
Games Workshop Web site: www.games-workshop.com
Forge World Web site: www.forgeworld.co.uk

>>> Subject: Event log shift 689 of the year of Him of Terra 996.M41.
>>> Conduit: Necro-vox KNN866.
>>> Thought for the Day: Righteous is the murder made in the name of the Emperor.

Subjects of Lord Helmawr, heed now the voice of Necromunda!

++ The Imperial House condemns the 0.013% drop in overall hab zone production, work clans are expected to take suitable measures to rectify this affront to the Emperor.
++ 8.7% Shortfalls in CS production in sectors Gamma 116-213 will be made up personally by Gamma work crews.
++ Hab Domes in Sector Theta 15 have been restored to 38% stability and are now deemed suitable for habitation.
++ House Goliath forge yield +2.5%, Embryo Farm production +1.1%.
++ Average authorised gang violence quotient +4.2%. Acceptable.
++ Average unauthorised gang violence quotient +23% (cf Increase in bounties re: mid-hive conflicts).

>> [Additional] Recent increases in the quotient of sanctioned Bounty Hunter contracts has precipitated an influx of 'scum' from throughout the hive. Helmawr applauds these enterprising individuals and encourages clan Houses and clan gangs to make use of these sanctioned soldiers of the Pax Imperia within the environs of Hive Primus and the Great Primus Hive Cluster.
>>> The Imperial House condemns the arrival of unsanctioned killers in the guise of Bounty Hunters. These debased individuals, who have chosen to ignore Helmawr's generous offer of legitimacy through the purchase of a contract, should be treated as the enemies of righteousness they are. For the Imperial House and the will of Him of Terra!

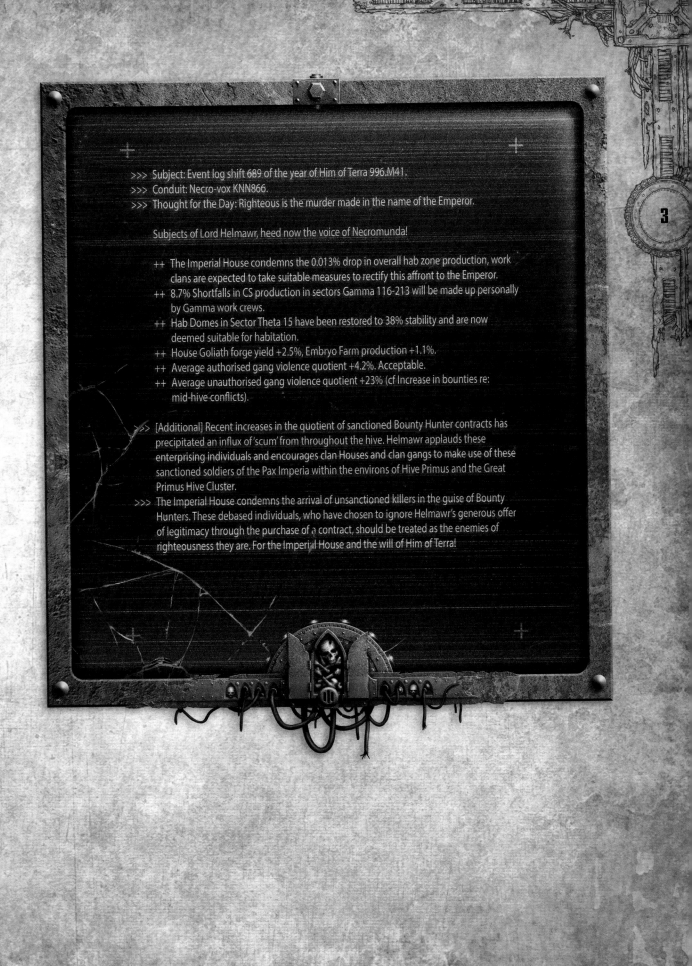

THE GANG WARS RAGE ON

Gang War Two is the second expansion for *Necromunda: Underhive* and adds a variety of new rules, weapons and fighters. Inside this book you will find rules to field the fighters of House Orlock to the tabletop, the gangers of the House of Iron bringing their own tactics and weapons to the battle for the underhive.

Gang War Two also introduces a new kind of fighter for your gangs – the Hired Gun. These hardened scummers can be contracted by your gangs, and provide well-equipped and skilled killers to bolster your gang's firepower. There are a variety of Hired Guns, including everything from steely-eyed Bounty Hunters to blood-spattered Rogue Docs.

To enhance your games and ramp up the danger, *Gang War Two* introduces a whole host of Underhive Perils, along with a collection of new gaming tiles compatible with the existing tunnel tiles from Necromunda: Underhive. These perils include collapsed tunnel sections, malfunctioning generatoriums, flooded passages and xenos nesting chambers to name but a few, each included with a full set of rules.

Also presented is an extensive Underhive Armoury which gathers together weapons, armour and gear from the Trading Post, House equipment lists and *Necromunda: Underhive*, as well as a reference section and Hired Gun stat cards.

DRAMATIS PERSONAE

Throughout this book, you will find illustrations of famous (or infamous) characters that your gangs can ally with or recruit, such as that on the opposite page. These are accompanied by details of their careers and a Fighter card showing their characteristics, skills and wargear. Players should feel free to photocopy these cards and cut them out, or transcribe the details onto a blank Fighter card. Many of these Dramatis Personae have profiles that are not possible to generate using the rules for creating your own Bounty Hunters in the Hired Guns and Hangers-on chapter. This is deliberate, to play up the character of these unique underhive denizens, and each will, in time, be represented by a highly detailed model.

GRENDL GRENDLSEN, SQUAT BOUNTY HUNTER

As a banner-jarl in the famed Vega Rams mercenary company, Grendl came to Necromunda with the Rogue Trader Lord Constant Gerrit of the Arcadius dynasty's guard of honour. But while his liege was entertained in the undreamed-of luxury of Lord Helmawr's spire-palace, the Abhuman members of his household, including the entire complement of the Vega Rams, were required to remain in the Stranger's Tower, as they were forbidden to set foot in the hive proper. In some ways, it is fortunate for Grendl that he was not present when the wing of the Helmawr Palace-spire in which Constant Gerrit was being housed was destroyed by a low-yield atomic charge planted by a rival House; yet in others it was unfortunate, for in the subsequent household purge, Grendl was forced to flee, seeking sanctuary in the anonymous squalor of the underhive.

Despite the dire circumstances of his coming to Hive Primus, Grendl Grendlsen quickly established a new life, finding gainful employ as a bodyguard to various underhive figures. At length, he earned the right to practice as a sanctioned Bounty Hunter, and now serves any master who will pay his fee. Grendl is famed for protecting his charges from their rivals and subsequently claiming the bounty on the would-be assassins' heads, and so far there has been no shortage of foolhardy rivals eager to test his skills, and his infamous hammer.

GRENDL GRENDLSEN, BOUNTY HUNTER — 280 CREDITS

M	WS	BS	S	T	W	I	A	Ld	Cl	Wil	Int
3"	3+	4+	3	4	3	5+	1	5+	7+	5+	5+

Weapon	Rng S	Rng L	Acc S	Acc L	Str	Ap	D	Am	Traits
Boltgun	12"	24"	+1	-	4	-1	2	6+	Rapid Fire (1)
Power hammer	-	E	-	-	+1	-1	2	-	Melee, Power
Frag grenades	-	Sx3	-	-	3	-	1	4+	Blast (3"), Grenade, Knockback

SKILLS: Combat Master, Iron Jaw, Nerves of Steel

WARGEAR: Armoured undersuit, flak armour

GANGS OF HOUSE ORLOCK

House Orlock is known throughout Necromunda as the 'House of Iron', an industrial superpower fuelled by countless ore mines and a stranglehold monopoly of the convoys serving the ferrous slag-heaps that lie out in the Ash Wastes. To the other Houses of Necromunda, Orlock seems as unified as a clenched fist, its gangers well-organised, equipped and utterly united in purpose. Life for the average serf of House Orlock is one of unending servitude, with each man and woman doomed to endless toil within the cramped confines of the ore pits and mines from which their masters derive their vast wealth. All thought of rebellion among the masses is purged from the herd by stony-faced overseers at the cracking tip of electro-goad and psi-whip, until nought but unthinking obedience remains. Compared to these bent-backed serfs, the men and women of Orlock's gangs walk proud and tall through the

smoke-clogged hallways of the House of Iron. To be an Orlock ganger is to have risen above the brutal drudgery of serfdom and claimed a life of violence and personal freedom in its stead. These are warriors born out of the fires of a vicious internal war, spoken of by the Orlocks as the 'Crucible Schism'.

More than a millennium ago, the crushing weight of House Orlock's oppressive regime caused its wretched serf-caste to rise up in open insurrection. Though appearing outwardly strong, the House had grown weak through complacency, and the soldiers of its levied militia were ill-prepared for the wrathful legions of raging foundry and mine-workers. Thousands died in the flames of rebellion and the outward facade of House Orlock's composure began to slip. Administratum-tithe enquiries were made and whispers of Adeptus Arbites investigations (and worse) began to circulate. Desperate, but cunning, the House masters worked a masterstroke that put down the rebellion by turning it upon itself. Propagandists went into overdrive, fomenting hatred of rival Houses in every shine-soaked drinking hole, while House militia units pulled back from their brutal riot control exercises and recruiters called on loyal Orlocks to unite for the good of all… and most importantly against the imaginary agents of the other Houses. One by one, bands of raging revolutionaries fell into line – and as they did so, they were armed and turned against those still in open rebellion. Now, between the nobility of the House's great families and the malcontent masses stood a core of fighters – hundreds of nascent gangs eager to carve out a chunk of Necromunda for themselves. The rebellion that had torn the underbelly from Orlock's industry in mere weeks was halted. It was the refiner's fire that produced the Iron House's greatest asset.

The relationship formed in the aftermath of the Crucible Schism remains in place centuries later. Every Orlock, no matter how lowly, looks to the gangers who saunter arrogantly among them with a mixture of envy, longing and fear. The gangs keep the masses in check, not merely by threat of violence, but through the hope of a better future – the 'nod' from a gang leader is the promise of a new life, away from electro-flails and endless toil. The role of the gangs stretches far beyond this basic perk, however, for they are the mailed fist of House Orlock in the constant skirmishes between the great Houses of Necromunda. They protect the vast ore convoys that ply the Ash Wastes as guards and outriders, ward off prying eyes from the monstrous slag deposits at hive-bottom, and patrol the dark tunnels that lead into rival territory.

Life in an Orlock gang is tough, for their warriors have none of the stimm-grown muscle of Goliath gangers, the murder-tech of House Van Saar or the poisons of the Escher. Instead, they rely on sturdy weapons stamped and pressed in the Orlock foundries, and a fighting spirit born from the House's us-against-them philosophy. In the drinking dens and gang houses of Orlock, every ganger is instilled with the warrior creed known as 'The Iron Brotherhood'. Put simply: *my gang before my House, my House before the rest.* This code is the way of life for every Orlock ganger, from the greenest Juve scalped from an ore-scraping line to the oldest Iron-touched shot-caller ready to head up-hive. Forget the code and a ganger ends up gutted, face-down in a sump-flow. Honour it, and their brothers and sisters will fight and die by their side.

This close-knit bond lends itself well to the Orlock methods of gang war. Orlocks pass openly through society, confident that their gang-kin have their backs at every turn. They carry sturdy autoguns, shotguns and stubbers, House-made and true-stamped. Reliability is sought after before all other factors, and it's said among the Orlocks that if a weapon doesn't spit lead stoppage-free, there's no place for it in the House of Iron – not that an Orlock won't take a trophy from a dead enemy, however. The irony of slaughtering a rival ganger with a weapon scavenged from the fallen has a poetry not lost on an Orlock's soul. With a ready supply of House-wrought weapons and munitions churned out by the House serfs, Orlock gangs are well-equipped to guard their territory. To do this, gangs typically form a network of 'friends' and accomplices who will warn them of encroachments onto their territories. This creates a loyalty among the local House serfs, who know that the loot plundered by the gangs will filter down to them, and they can expect first pickings after the gangers themselves.

Every Orlock gang has its own idiosyncrasies and traditions, but many style themselves after the notorious Iron Skulls, a sprawling gang who rose up in the wake of the Crucible Schism. The founder of the Iron Skulls was once a down-hive slag miner known as Cheros Jal. Jal's warriors carved out territory bordering with the Delaques in Hive Trazior over the course of several years and their actions helped foment the bitter rivalry with House Delaque that remains to this day.

Jal's greatest fame stems from the 'Ashline Heist', during which he and his outriders captured a Delaque armoured train and used it to smash apart the clan's grand pipeline nexus. The Delaque power in Trazior faded and House Orlock was able to wrest the much-coveted Ulanti contract from them. For three decades thereafter, Jal and his Iron Skulls ruled a swathe of Trazior that was the envy of all around them. Hounded at every turn by the murder-squads of House Delaque, the Iron Skulls became masters of ambush, maintaining a constant state of readiness that leaves them credited with the 'full fist' principle – no Orlock ganger travels alone, or without a gun in their hand. Jal's final fate is unknown. Some say he died outnumbered, fighting beside his crew, others that he wandered grey-haired and old into the Ash Wastes to seek their fate. Regardless, even now, Orlock gangers still speak of him in awed tones and many look to the Iron Skulls as the exemplars of what it means to be a ganger in the House of Iron.

SHOTGUN JACK
SUMP DOGS
HOUSE ORLOCK

HOUSE ORLOCK GANGS

GANG COMPOSITION

An Orlock gang must follow these rules when it is founded, and when new fighters are added to the gang:

- There must be one Leader (if the Leader is killed, see page 24 of *Gang War*).
- There can be no more than two Champions, plus one for every full 10 Reputation the gang has – for example, a gang with Reputation 24 could have up to four Champions.
- The total number of Gangers in the gang must be equal to or higher than the total number of other fighters (Leaders, Juves and Champions) in the gang, not counting Hangers-on (see page 16).
- A fighter can be equipped with a maximum of three weapons. Weapons with the Unwieldy trait take up the space of two weapons – these are marked with an asterisk (*) in the equipment list.

SKILL ACCESS

Orlock fighters have access to the following skills (see page 41):

	Agility	Brawn	Combat	Cunning	Ferocity	Leadership	Shooting	Savant
Leader	-	Secondary	-	-	Primary	Primary	Secondary	Primary
Champion	-	Secondary	-	-	Primary	Secondary	Secondary	Primary
Juve	-	-	-	-	Primary	-	Secondary	Secondary
Specialist	-	Secondary	-	-	Primary	-	Secondary	Primary

"My crew before my House, my House before the rest."

From the 'Iron Brotherhood', Orlock gang creed

FIGHTERS

A starting Orlock gang is made up of the following fighters:

LEADER .... 120 CREDITS

M	WS	BS	S	T	W	I	A	Ld	Cl	Wil	Int
5"	3+	3+	3	3	3	4+	2	4+	5+	5+	5+

EQUIPMENT

An Orlock Leader is equipped with mesh armour. They have no equipment restrictions.

STARTING SKILL

Orlock Leaders start with one skill chosen from their Primary skill sets.

CHAMPIONS .... 95 CREDITS EACH

M	WS	BS	S	T	W	I	A	Ld	Cl	Wil	Int
5"	4+	3+	3	3	2	4+	2	5+	6+	6+	6+

EQUIPMENT

An Orlock Champion is equipped with mesh armour. They have no equipment restrictions.

STARTING SKILL

Orlock Champions start with one skill chosen from their Primary skill sets.

JUVES .... 30 CREDITS EACH

M	WS	BS	S	T	W	I	A	Ld	Cl	Wil	Int
6"	5+	5+	3	3	1	3+	1	7+	8+	8+	8+

EQUIPMENT

An Orlock Juve starts with no equipment. They can be equipped with Pistols and Close Combat Weapons, but cannot be given any weapon that is worth more than 20 credits.

GANGERS .... 55 CREDITS EACH

M	WS	BS	S	T	W	I	A	Ld	Cl	Wil	Int
5"	4+	4+	3	3	1	4+	1	6+	7+	7+	7+

EQUIPMENT

An Orlock Ganger is equipped with mesh armour. They can be equipped with Basic Weapons, Close Combat Weapons, Grenades, Pistols and Wargear.

HOUSE ORLOCK HARPOON LAUNCHER

The harpoon launcher is designed for use by House outriders escorting ore convoys across the Ash Wastes of Necromunda. It is ideal for taking down enemy vehicle crew while leaving their vehicle undamaged and ripe for capture, or for setting lines at head-height across a road to behead the exposed crew of bikes and light vehicles. As many Orlock gangers are veterans of such expeditions into the Ash Wastes, they greatly value the harpoon launcher, as much as a status symbol as a useful weapon to take to a gang fight.

HOUSE ORLOCK EQUIPMENT LIST
WEAPONS

BASIC WEAPONS
- Sawn-off shotgun .... 10 credits
- Autogun .... 15 credits
- Shotgun (with solid and scatter ammo) .... 30 credits
- Combat shotgun (with salvo and shredder ammo) .... 60 credits

CLOSE COMBAT WEAPONS
- Fighting knife .... 10 credits
- Servo-claw .... 30 credits

PISTOLS
- Stub gun .... 5 credits
- Autopistol .... 10 credits

HEAVY WEAPONS
- Harpoon launcher .... 110 credits
- Heavy stubber* .... 130 credits

GRENADES
- Frag grenades .... 30 credits
- Krak grenades .... 45 credits
- Blasting charges .... 45 credits

WARGEAR
- Filter plugs .... 10 credits
- Strip kit .... 15 credits
- Photo-goggles .... 30 credits
- Respirator .... 15 credits

COMBAT SHOTGUN, HOUSE ORLOCK

DRUM FED AUTOPISTOL, HOUSE ORLOCK

HARPOON LAUNCHER (CHEST PIERCER), HOUSE ORLOCK

FIGHTING KNIFE, HOUSE ORLOCK

STUB GUN, HOUSE ORLOCK MASS MANUFACTURE

NAMING YOUR OWN ORLOCKS

While it might seem a trivial thing, it is in fact vitally important to name each of your gangers (after all, how will their deeds live on after their deaths if their names are unknown!). Below are some elements that can be used individually or combined to name gangers aligned to the House of Iron.

- Grimm
- Ironhead
- Nark
- Groff
- Fast
- Don
- Rock
- Thorson
- Jo
- Silent
- Sour
- Fist
- Gann
- Red
- Zeke
- Lander
- Mo
- Radder
- Crow
- Duster

HIRED GUNS AND HANGERS-ON

This section introduces new types of fighters that can be used in both campaigns and skirmish battles, broadly defined as 'Hired Guns' (mercenaries that will help a gang out in the short term for pay) and 'Hangers-on' (trusted associates of the gang who offer services other than fighting). More types of Hired Gun and Hangers-on will be introduced in future Necromunda supplements.

Hired Guns and Hangers-on can add a lot to a gang. When attached to a newly-founded gang they, can make up for certain gaps in skills and equipment the gang might have. But more than that, they lend a lot of character and narrative, as well as serving as an opportunity for modellers to really go to town painting and converting miniatures to match their vision of these often highly idiosyncratic characters.

HIRED GUNS

In campaign play, gangs have the chance to recruit Hired Guns in the pre-battle sequence (see page 20 in *Gang War*); this secures their services for that one battle. They are not added to the gang roster, but a Fighter card will need to be filled out for them. They can be hired again for subsequent battles – as such, players might find it useful to keep an appropriate Fighter card, already filled in, for each Hired Gun model they have.

Hired Guns never gain Experience, they cannot purchase Advancements, and they do not suffer Lasting Injuries – if they go Out of Action, they simply play no further part in the battle. Also, no additional equipment can be added to their Fighter card, aside from what is listed in their entry below.

In skirmish battles, Hired Guns can be purchased in the same way as any other fighter.

In either mode of play, a Hired Gun increases the gang's Rating in the same way as any other fighter.

HIVE SCUM ....30 CREDITS
Hive Scum, or Scummers, are masterless or itinerant hivers who will fight for anyone who offers them coin. Many are drunkards and down-and-outs, but even these have their uses and despite appearances, are quite capable of holding their own in a fight. Others are mercenaries who travel from zone to zone, making few friends or commitments, earning whatever easy money is around before moving on. Scum are too wild and independent to submit to the leadership of anyone for very long, and they hire out their services as they feel like it. Despite their carefree lifestyle and happy-go-lucky attitude, Scummers are good fighters, so their services are always in demand. Many end up working for the Guilders, but there are always a few willing to tag along with a gang for a share of the spoils.

Hive Scum are especially valuable to a newly-founded gang, especially one whose fighters may be neither numerous nor especially experienced. In general, more established gangs eschew their services, preferring to rely on their own in the heat of battle. Nonetheless, Hive Scum are considered of great value as cannon fodder...

A gang can recruit up to five Hive Scum at a time.

M	WS	BS	S	T	W	I	A	Ld	Cl	Wil	Int
5"	4+	4+	3	3	1	4+	1	8+	8+	8+	8+

EQUIPMENT
The Hive Scum may be equipped with up to 60 credits' worth of equipment, purchased from the Pistols, Close Combat Weapons and Basic Weapons sections of the Trading Post. They may be armed with up to three weapons. Only one weapon may have the Unwieldy Weapon Trait, and this counts as two weapons choices.

"Listen, stop struggling – your life's over... if they don't just stretch your neck, they're gonna ship you off to the slave-gangs. If you think downhive is hell, you ain't seen nothing yet."

Lodian Kreel,
Sanctioned
Bounty Hunter

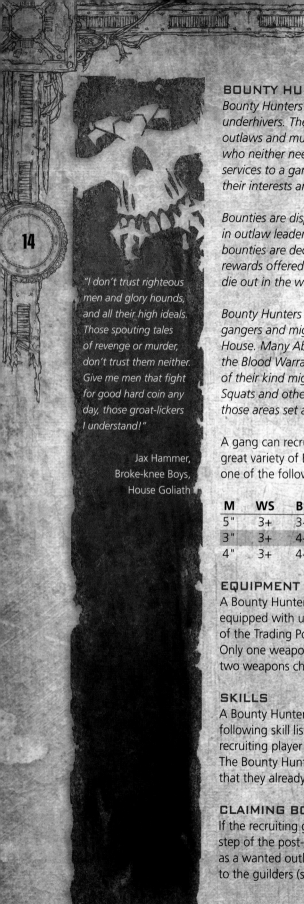

BOUNTY HUNTER ....80 CREDITS

Bounty Hunters are amongst the toughest and most dangerous of all Necromunda underhivers. They survive in perilous conditions, living out in the wastes, pursuing outlaws and mutants through the tunnels and ruins. Bounty Hunters are loners who neither need, nor want, to be associated with a gang. They will hire their services to a gang leader though if there are no decent bounties to be had or if their interests are aligned, but such allegiances tend to be temporary.

Bounties are displayed at all Trading Posts, offering rewards to anyone who brings in outlaw leaders, gangs, mutants and other criminal types. Sometimes, general bounties are declared on Ratskin Renegades or on underhive monsters. The rewards offered are good, but the job is a perilous one and many Bounty Hunters die out in the wastes, slain by the outlaws and mutants they set out to hunt.

Bounty Hunters are drawn from a wide range of backgrounds. Some are erstwhile gangers and might still bear some of the distinctive trappings of their former Clan House. Many Abhumans also find the life of a Bounty Hunter suits them well, for the Blood Warrant that serves as license and writ allows them to go where others of their kind might ordinarily be barred. Thus it is not uncommon to see Beastmen, Squats and other stable Abhuman strains operating as Bounty Hunters far from those areas set aside for their kind.

A gang can recruit no more than one Bounty Hunter at a time. To represent the great variety of Bounty Hunters active on Necromunda, the recruiting player picks one of the following profiles to use.

M	WS	BS	S	T	W	I	A	Ld	Cl	Wil	Int
5"	3+	3+	3	3	2	3+	1	7+	5+	6+	6+
3"	3+	4+	3	4	2	5+	1	5+	7+	5+	5+
4"	3+	4+	3	4	1	4+	2	7+	6+	7+	8+

EQUIPMENT

A Bounty Hunter has either flak armour or mesh armour and in addition may be equipped with up to 150 credits' worth of equipment purchased from any sections of the Trading Post. A Bounty Hunter may be armed with up to five weapons. Only one weapon may have the Unwieldy Weapon Trait, and this counts as two weapons choices.

SKILLS

A Bounty Hunter has three skills. Each is chosen at random from one of the following skill lists: Agility, Brawn, Combat, Cunning, Ferocity, or Shooting. The recruiting player picks one skill list, rolls for the skill, then picks the next, and so on. The Bounty Hunter can have multiple skills from the same list; if they obtain a skill that they already have, it must be re-rolled.

CLAIMING BOUNTIES

If the recruiting gang captures an enemy fighter, roll a D6 in the Receive Rewards step of the post-battle sequence. On a 6, the Bounty Hunter recognises the captive as a wanted outlaw. Mark this on the capturing gang's roster. If the captive is sold to the guilders (see page 23 in *Gang War*), they receive an additional D6x10 credits.

YOLANDA SKORN, BOUNTY HUNTER

There is usually little mercy for gangers who challenge their leaders and fail, and most end their days rotting at the bottom of the Sump. Sometimes, though, a rival is so impressive, simple execution seems like a waste. This was the case for the Escher Bounty Hunter Yolanda Skorn. The leader of her former gang, the Bloodmaidens, looked into her crazed eyes, even as she grinned through sheets of blood from her freshly carved exile scars and decided nothing so cruel and beautiful could be taken from the world.

Skorn's missing hand, lost in the duel, was replaced with a whirring cybernetic, and she adopted a veil to hide her facial scars (mostly so they didn't unsettle her allies), before setting off on a journey of murder and mayhem. As anyone who has met her will attest, Skorn is quite insane. She constantly talks to her weapons, doors, the walls and anything else that crosses her path. She also enjoys close-in kills, sometimes pulling aside her veil so her enemies can see her scars 'smile' before they die. Understandably, Yolanda Skorn's reputation precedes her most places she goes, and the mere sight of her can send some enemies running. It also means she seldom stays with the one employer for long, as there is only so many times a gang leader can wake up with Skorn's staring eyes an inch from their face before deciding that enough is enough.

YOLANDA SKORN, BOUNTY HUNTER

230 CREDITS

M	WS	BS	S	T	W	I	A	Ld	Cl	Wil	Int
5"	3+	3+	3	3	2	3+	2	7+	5+	6+	6+

	Rng		Acc						
Weapon	S	L	S	L	Str	Ap	D	Am	Traits
Stiletto knife	-	E	-	+1	S	-	1		Melee, Toxin
Stub gun	6"	12"	+2	-	3	-	1	4+	Pistol, Plentiful
Frag grenades	-	Sx3	-	-	3	-	1	4+	Blast (3"), Grenade, Knockback

SKILLS: Counter-attack, Fearsome, Parry

WARGEAR: Flak armour, photo-googles, respirator

HANGERS-ON

Once a gang establishes itself, its hideout can become as well-known as any other local landmark. Some gangs' hideouts become centres of activity, with loyal hivers granted the freedom to come and go as they please, while others are more like fortresses. In either case, they are sought-after destinations for merchants and tradesmen seeking a reliable base of operations and offering their services to the gang.

Hangers-on are primarily used in campaign play. In the Update Roster step of the post-battle sequence, players can recruit Hangers-on. These are purchased with credits from the gang's Stash, in the same way as new fighters. A Fighter card is filled out for them and they are added to the gang roster. Most Hangers-on have various options for their equipment – these must be decided when they are recruited.

'MONO', PORT MAD DOG LONGSHOREMAN AND OCCASIONAL MERC

The maximum number of Hangers-on a gang can have is limited by their Reputation, as shown by the table below. If a gang's Reputation drops to the point that they do not have enough for their Hangers-on, they must remove one or more of them from their roster until they are back within their limit. Also, note that there is a limit on each type of Hanger-on – a gang can have up to two Rogue Docs, but only one Dome Runner. Hangers-on do not count towards the number of fighters in the gang; for example, they are not counted when determining how many Gangers the gang must contain.

Reputation	Maximum Hangers-on
Less than 5	0
5-9	1
10-14	2
15-19	3
20-24	4
Each additional 5	+1

Each of the types of Hangers-on gives a gang a special rule, but they do not normally take part in battles. However, whenever a battle happens on the gang's turf (i.e., they have the Home Turf Advantage in a scenario), roll a D6 for each of their Hangers-on before choosing a crew. On a result of 1, 2 or 3, the Hanger-on is unfortunate enough to be around when the fighting starts, and must be included as part of the crew. Hangers-on cannot gain Experience or Advancements; if they suffer a Lasting Injury that would make a change to their Fighter card, they decide that the hideout is no longer safe and move on – they are removed from the gang roster. They also cannot be given any equipment other than what is listed.

HANGERS-ON IN SKIRMISH BATTLES

Hangers-on are primarily designed for campaign play, but they can also be used in skirmish battles when playing a scenario in which the defender has the Home Turf Advantage (see page 52 in *Gang War*). They do not cost any credits when used in this way; instead, the defender rolls a D3, and can include up to that many Hangers-on in their crew.

0-2 ROGUE DOCS ....50 CREDITS

Medical expertise is much sought-after in the underhive, and most of those who have such training sell their services at a not insignificant price. However, should tragedy befall one of these 'docs' – perhaps an influential gang leader dies under their scalpel, or they are blamed for an outbreak of sickness – they will throw in their lot with a friendly gang, trading their expertise for protection.

If a gang has a Rogue Doc, it can make an additional Medical Escort action in the post-battle sequence (see page 23 in *Gang War*) in addition to any other actions made by the gang's Leader or Champions. This visit does not cost any credits – however, a result of 6 on the table is treated as Stabilised rather than a Full Recovery, thanks to the Doc's comparatively limited supplies and the lack of proper medical technology. If a gang has more than one Rogue Doc, it can make this additional action once for each of them.

M	WS	BS	S	T	W	I	A	Ld	Cl	Wil	Int
5"	5+	5+	2	3	1	4+	1	9+	8+	7+	5+

EQUIPMENT
Laspistol or stub gun, medicae kit

SKILLS
Medicae

0-3 AMMO-JACKS ....50 CREDITS

As gangs become more experienced, they discover the importance of regular weapon checks. Running out of ammunition or suffering a gun jam in the middle of a firefight is just not acceptable for a gang that wishes to be taken seriously. As such, many take on full-time armourers, setting up a workshop within their hideout to ensure that such mishaps are far less likely.

If a gang has an Ammo-jack, its weapons are regularly serviced and their ammo stocks are carefully maintained. As such, fighters from the gang can re-roll any failed Ammo checks that roll a natural 1. The Ammo-jack does not have to take part in the battle for the gang to receive this bonus, but if they are not available for the battle, for example, if they are In Recovery or have been Captured, the bonus does not apply.

If a gang has more than one Ammo-jack, the bonus increases. A gang with two Ammo-jacks can re-roll failed Ammo checks that roll a natural 1 or 2. A gang with three can re-roll failed Ammo checks that roll a natural 1, 2 or 3.

M	WS	BS	S	T	W	I	A	Ld	Cl	Wil	Int
5"	4+	3+	3	3	1	5+	1	9+	7+	6+	7+

EQUIPMENT
Boltgun or combat shotgun with salvo and scatter ammo; power hammer or power sword; mesh armour

SKILLS
Munitioneer

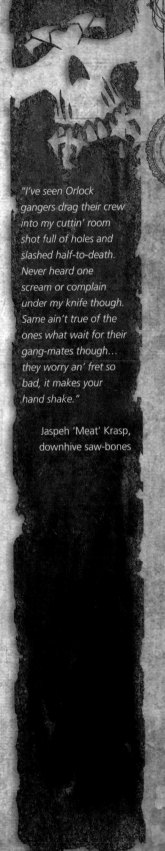

"I've seen Orlock gangers drag their crew into my cuttin' room shot full of holes and slashed half-to-death. Never heard one scream or complain under my knife though. Same ain't true of the ones what wait for their gang-mates though… they worry an' fret so bad, it makes your hand shake."

Jaspeh 'Meat' Krasp, downhive saw-bones

EYROS SLAGMYST, ENHANCED BOUNTY HUNTER

Eyros was once an underhive dome-rigger from Cogtown, one of the sweating, emaciated souls responsible for repairing the rusting pipe networks that fed the dismal settlement. When the Eye-Blight came to Cogtown, and its population began to die, Eyros and a group of dome-riggers set off into the underhive to find the scrap-tech to save their town. Deep down in the sump wells, close to hive bottom, the scavenging party found a vault of hidden treasures, among them a wondrous contraption that could extract life-giving water from almost anything. It was Eyros who donned the strange archaeo-rig, its syringes and bone-flutes burrowing into his flesh until all his organs pulsed in time with the machine. Unfortunately for Eyros, though it gave him strength and life, it also gave him a burning thirst.

As it turned out, while water can be found in many things, few things in Necromunda have quite as much as humans. After Eyros had drained his companions, he returned to Cogtown and left only dust and scrap in his wake. He soon discovered that the potent fluids concocted in the harness could also be dispensed to his allies, and it was not long before Eyros began selling his services and 'water' to gangs in exchange for fresh subjects to drink from. These days it is hard to tell how much of Eyros is left under the archaeo-cybernetics that have taken root within him, his features hidden under writhing wires and pitted armour. There is also no telling what Eyros will become once the archaeotech is done with him.

EYROS SLAGMYST, BOUNTY HUNTER — 270 CREDITS

M	WS	BS	S	T	W	I	A	LD	CL	WIL	INT
4"	3+	4+	3	4	2	5+	1	5+	7+	5+	5+

Weapon	Rng S	Rng L	Acc S	Acc L	Str	Ap	D	Am	Traits
Laspistol	8"	12"	+1	-	3	-	1	2+	Pistol, Plentiful
Frag grenades	-	Sx3	-	-	3	-	1	4+	Blast (3"), Grenade, Knockback
Fighting knife	-	E	-	-	S	-1	1	-	Backstab, Melee

SKILLS: Ironjaw, True Grit, Nerves of Steel

WARGEAR: Armoured undersuit, bio-booster, furnace plates, medicae kit, photo-googles

0-1 DOME RUNNER ....20 CREDITS

A gang's Turf is its primary source of income, but as it expands outwards, the gangers might find themselves in areas they've never even visited. Local guides, referred to as 'Dome Runners', are a regular sight among gangs wishing to root out this new turf's hidden treasures. Runners come from a variety of backgrounds, generally unfortunate, but they all have one thing in common: an exhaustive knowledge of the local area and a distinct lack of other marketable skills. From stick-thin waifs to gnarled ex-gangers, these vagabonds gladly settle down with a gang in exchange for reliable shelter.

When a gang with a Dome Runner gains or steals Turf (see page 23 in *Gang War*), add 1 to the roll to see whether they gain a new Special Territory. In addition, when they gain a Special Territory, the controlling player can choose to reverse the order of the D66 roll (for example, turning a 36 into a 63).

M	WS	BS	S	T	W	I	A	Ld	Cl	Wil	Int
5"	5+	5+	3	3	1	3+	1	10+	9+	7+	8+

EQUIPMENT
Laspistol or stub gun; fighting knife or axe

SKILLS
Lie Low

0-1 SLOPPER ....20 CREDITS

Food in the underhive rarely holds any joy. Most meals consist of corpse-starch or nutri-slime, supplemented with synth-fats and vitamin shots. As such, anyone who can produce 'real' food from the local flora and fauna can expect a steady stream of credits. They are usually keen to set up a kitchen in a gang's headquarters; they get somewhere secure to store their wares, and the gang gets its share of leftovers.

At the end of the Spend Experience step of the pre-battle sequence, roll a D6 for each of the gang's fighters that is In Recovery. On a roll of 6, a constant supply of good food has helped them recover more quickly – their In Recovery box on the gang roster is cleared, and are now available for this battle.

M	WS	BS	S	T	W	I	A	Ld	Cl	Wil	Int
4"	4+	4+	2	3	1	3+	1	9+	9+	5+	7+

EQUIPMENT
Fighting knife

SKILLS
None

"What, you're too good for a bowl of vent-scrapings? Just wait 'til the old belly-flukes hatch, then you'll soon get it down you – wriggly bits and all!"

Oblat Three-tooth,
Scrapfalls Slopper

UNDERHIVE PERILS

This section presents rules for additional Necromunda: Underhive Zone Mortalis board sections, available as a separately sold pack. Players can agree to use them when setting up a Zone Mortalis battle, adding them to the tiles that are available. If players wish to use them for the scenarios in the *Necromunda: Underhive* rulebook, they can either create an entirely new board layout or substitute an Underhive Perils tile for one that already contains a peril (such as a pitfall or toxic sludge).

CULT RITUAL CHAMBER

No world in the vast Imperium is immune to the taint of the Ruinous Powers, and on Necromunda its touch is as likely to be felt in the gilded salons of the spire-palaces as it is in the nighted domes of the underhive and in the overcrowded hab zones in between. Cultists of the Chaos gods often hide their ritual gatherings by meeting in sectors entombed by rubble and waste from the upper levels or accessible only through hidden openings. Those who discover such chambers are often driven insane by unheard ramblings and scarred by unseen hands. Those few who escape unharmed and with their sanity intact are considered the fortunate ones, no matter how scared they may be from witnessing their fellows being slowly corrupted by the laughter of thirsting gods...

RITUAL CIRCLE

UNDERHIVE PERILS IN SECTOR MECHANICUS BATTLES

Many of the perils found here can be adapted for use in Sector Mechanicus battles. In many cases, this is simply a case of creating a bespoke piece of terrain to represent them; however, if any additional guidelines are needed, they will be found in a box-out next to the relevant entry.

If a fighter ends their turn within 6" of the Ritual Circle, make a Willpower check for them. If the check is failed, an Insanity marker is placed on the fighter's card (these can be found on the Underhive Perils token sheet).

If a fighter has an Insanity marker when they are activated, roll a D6:

On a 1 or 2, they immediately become Broken – or, if they were already Broken, they flee the battlefield (even if their gang has not failed a Bottle test).

On a 3 or 4, the opposing player can control that fighter this turn, treating them as part of their gang, for example, they could charge or shoot at another fighter from the insane fighter's gang, treating them as an enemy. Once the turn is over, the fighter no longer counts as part of the opposing gang.

On a 5 or 6, the fighter can act as normal. Once their turn is over, make a Willpower check for them; if it is passed, they lose their Insanity marker.

IN SECTOR MECHANICUS...

When setting up terrain in a Sector Mechanicus battle, a suitable piece of scenery (perhaps an idol or altar) can be used in place of the Ritual Circle.

COLLAPSED SECTIONS

While the metres-thick flooring plates of the hive are constructed to remain strong for thousands of years, some sections are often subjected to the touch harshly corrosive chemicals, the natural traffic of a trade hub or recreational facility or, particularly on the lower levels, cataclysmic hive quakes. Events such as these force entire sectors to be abandoned, thus furthering the growth of the hive as it builds ever skyward. However this section collapsed, the river of waste from the upper hive has already begun to fill the mostly abandoned lower section and solidify around the fallen ruins in the hive's twisted self-regeneration. While such abandoned sections can prove valuable to the various gangs that pillage the depths of the hive, these collapsed floors have caused the downfall of entire gangs as the already-weakened floor gives way to their undignified deaths below.

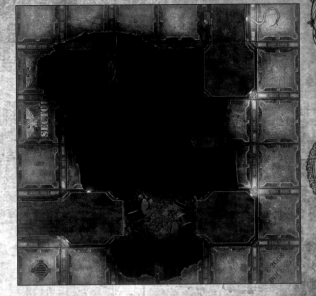

A Collapsed Section features one or more large Pitfalls, which follow the rules in the *Necromunda: Underhive* rulebook. In addition, if a weapon with the Blast trait is used and the centre of the Blast marker ends on a Collapsed Section tile, make an Initiative test for each fighter on that tile. If the test is failed, the floor shifts and the fighter is moved D3" towards the nearest Pitfall (potentially falling if they move into it).

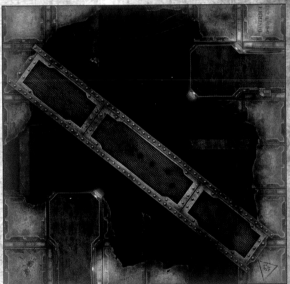

ARCHAEOTECH DEVICE

The sprawl of tunnels that runs the breadth of the underhive is dotted with examples of ancient technology, some of it still working. Often found in chambers bedecked with icons and sigils unknown to all but the adepts of the Mechanicus, these relics are valuable resources for any gang with an interest in technology – or with an interest in extorting credits from technology. In most cases these chambers would have been hidden behind multiple security measures, and possibly only accessible by the Mechanicus or other apprentices sufficiently blessed to enter, but in the ancient press of the lower hive such measures have long-since been forgotten. Miraculously, some such devices still seem to function, a sign of either the Omnissiah's continued blessing or, more likely, a valuable hidden power source.

CONSOLE   PLATFORM

An Active fighter within 1" of the Console can make the following action:

ACTIVATE DEVICE (BASIC) – Make an Intelligence check for the fighter. If it is passed, any weapons carried by any fighter who is currently standing at least partially on the Platform gain the Shock trait for the rest of the battle. If the check is failed, any fighter who is currently standing at least partially on the Platform is Pinned, then takes D6 Strength 2 hits with the Shock trait.

IN SECTOR MECHANICUS...

The piece of terrain representing the Archaeotech Device should have a Console; if it does not, a Door Terminal can be placed adjacent to the device to count as the Console. If the Device does not have a 'Platform' or something similar, the Activate Console action affects any fighters within 3" of the Device.

FURNACE FLOOR

A completely functional furnace in the underhive is a rare amenity, more so if it isn't claimed by one of House Goliath's many gangs. These facilities are prized objectives for any gang looking to extract a deal with House Goliath. Even when contaminated with human remains, effluent or general waste from the hive above, such furnaces have become central to many inter-gang power struggles as deadly torture chambers, disposal units or even to curry favour with House Goliath or those in service to the Great House.

FURNACE

VENTILATION TUNNEL

Even when the underhive was inhabited and functional, air from the less toxic levels of the atmosphere had to be pumped down to the lower levels. As these tunnels and ducts were designed to function in low-power environments, in cases of natural disasters, sabotage and industrial failings, most of these systems remain functional, even among sectors that have completely collapsed. However, given their size, these tunnels can make an entire corridor impassable – many an unfortunate ganger or scavie have been caught by the airflow and drawn into the blades, and now few dare to move even a footstep closer than they must to pass.

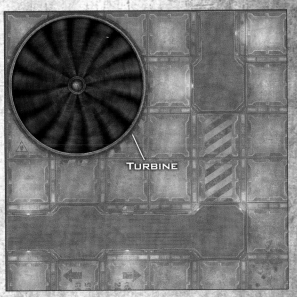

TURBINE

The Open Furnace is treated in the same way as a Pitfall. However, if a fighter is moved into the Furnace, no Initiative check is made for them – they immediately go Out of Action. Fighters who go Prone within 1" of the Furnace can still make an Initiative check. In a campaign battle, no Lasting Injury roll is made; this automatically counts as a 61-65 (Critical Injury).

In addition, the heat haze is such that any ranged attacks made across the Open Furnace have an additional -1 to hit modifier.

If a fighter ends an action within 6" of the Turbine, roll a D6 for them and add their Strength. If the result is 7 or more, their turn ends as they brace against the rushing wind. If the result is lower, they are moved D3" towards the centre of the Turbine and their turn ends.

If a fighter moves into the Turbine, they go Out of Action immediately. In campaign battles, make D3 Lasting Injury rolls instead of one.

In addition, if a Scatter dice is rolled for a Blast marker whose centre is within 6" of the Turbine), do not roll the Scatter dice – instead, the marker scatters towards the centre of the Turbine.

MALFUNCTIONING GENERATORIUM

The hives of Necromunda are ever-hungry for raw power to drive the ceaseless engines of industry, and once activated, a generator is rarely deactivated, instead functioning until such time as it fails and another is built to make up for the shortfall incurred by its failure. Abandoned by their tech-cult custodians, such generators may still be of use to a gang which is bold or foolish enough to attempt to harness the unchained energies they yet produce.

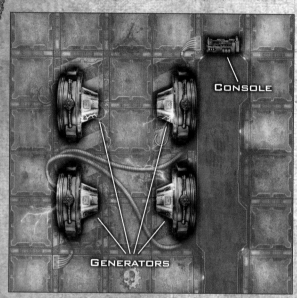

CONSOLE

GENERATORS

The Generators on this tile block line of sight in the same way as obstacles. While the Generators are active (i.e., they have not been deactivated as described below), if a fighter moves between two Generators or ends an action within 1" of a Generator, they are Pinned, their turn ends and they suffer D3 Strength 4 hits with the Shock trait.

A fighter within 1" of the Console can make the following action:

DEACTIVATE GENERATORS (BASIC) – Make an Intelligence check for the fighter. If it is passed, the Generators are deactivated until the end of the round.

SLUDGE FARM

A derogatory title used by underhivers to describe any area of unidentifiable and unpleasant biological run-off from such vital processes as corpse-starch processing, effluent refining or bulk mycoprotein cultivation, the area is foul-smelling and dangerous. Yet as with most things in the underhive, as potentially valuable as they are perilous.

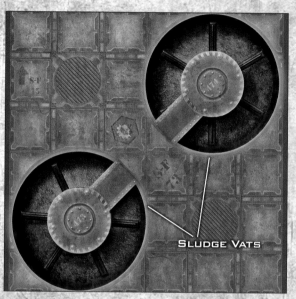

SLUDGE VATS

Sludge Vats follow the rules for Pitfalls; however, a model that falls into a Sludge Vat is not taken Out of Action. Instead, they are Pinned and moved into the vat, and if it is their turn, it ends immediately. Next time they take a turn, they must spend their entire turn climbing out of the Vat (move them the shortest distance possible); they are then Pinned.

Note that the Sludge Vats on this tile are set into the ground, and as such do not block line of sight.

FLOODED PASSAGE

While the uphive nobles sip on water imported at staggering expense from sources across the galaxy, downhivers must rely upon liquids recycled countless thousands of times over. The expense of a single flute of quantum-spun Cthellian ice-water would purchase sufficient liquid to sustain the workforce of an entire furnace zone for a whole shift. Even recyc water has value in the underhives however, and some gangs sabotage vital pipelines and infrastructure as acts of petty sabotage against larger gangs and Clan Houses, or set elaborate traps using live power cords or acidic compounds.

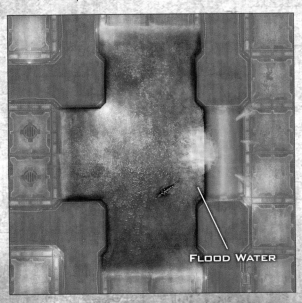

FLOOD WATER

If a Seriously Injured fighter ends an action in the Flood Water, roll a D6. On a 1, their injuries are too great to keep their head above water – the fighter immediately goes Out of Action.

SEWAGE CHANNEL

One of the staples of the diet fed to the industrial serfs of the Clan Houses is bulk mycoprotein, a foodstuff derived from fungus grown on the single most plentiful source of protein available in the hives. A constant stream of this source flows downwards to feed the mycoprotein plants, and many gangs use such channels as ideal ambush points or as a convenient means of disposing of the corpse of a scragged rival.

OPEN SEWER

If a fighter moves into the Open Sewer, or starts an action in the Open Sewer, roll a D6 and add their Strength. If the result is 7 or more, the fighter maintains their footing. If the result is lower, they are Pinned – or, if they are already Prone, they are swept away by the fast-flowing current and go Out of Action.

PROMETHIUM CACHE

Most gangs in the underhive hoard scavenged materials in hidden corners. These caches can contain anything from food to munitions, but if a firefight breaks out around a promethium stockpile, it's only a matter of time before a stray shot leads to a massive fireball.

The promethium barrels and storage tank on this tile can be targeted by ranged attacks as though they were fighters (they can also be hit by templates, Blast markers and stray shots – see page 58 of the *Necromunda: Underhive* rulebook). If the barrels and tanks are hit, roll a D6 and apply the attacking weapon's Armour Penetration value. On a result of 4 or more, the shot is deflected safely, but on a lower result, a barrel or the tank is breached and there is a huge detonation.

Every fighter within 3" of a barrel or the storage tank is immediately Pinned, and suffers a Strength 5 hit with a Damage of 2 and the Blaze trait. Once there has been a detonation, the barrels and storage tanks can no longer be hit – however, the space they occupied, and the Spilled Fuel, are ablaze for the rest of the battle. If a fighter moves into the blaze, they suffer a Strength 5 hit with a Damage of 2 and the Blaze trait.

BARRELS AND FUEL TANK

FUEL SPILL

UNLIT CORRIDORS

Inevitably, generators fail and wiring corrodes, plunging entire sections of the hive into darkness. Lightless corridors can present both a blessing and a curse to gangs in any given sector. While some welcome the darkness and use it as an opportunity to spring elaborate ambushes, cover the setting of booby traps or make their escape, other, typically less experienced gangs foolishly stumble into such traps laid for them in the dark.

Effect: If a fighter is standing in the shadows, they cannot be targeted by ranged attacks or spotted by sentries from more than 3" away unless they have a Blaze marker, or the attacker/sentry is using photo-goggles or an infra-scope. Additionally, add 1 to the dice roll to see whether a booby trap is triggered if it is within the shadows.

SECURE VAULT

As the hives grow ever upwards, once invaluable assets are abandoned and reclaimed by others. A secure vault might once have housed the wealth sufficient to purchase an entire world, and a still functioning example is of huge value to any underhive gang that can keep hold of it. They may serve as prisons, torture chambers, boltholes or armouries, for once locked from within, they are all-but impervious to intrusion.

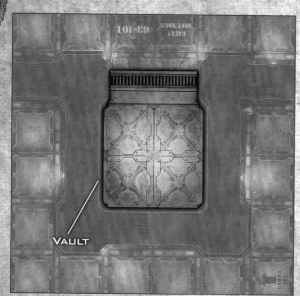

VAULT

FUNGUS SPRAWL

The underhives of Necromunda are host to all manner of bizarre mutant flora, with some long-abandoned domes being entirely overrun by twisted forests of weirdly-glowing fungal forms, the air thick with choking clouds of drifting spores. None can say how such strains come into existence, but as with most things in the underhive, they are often put to use by those who live there, in most cases as food, medicine or lethal poison.

When setting up the Secure Vault tile, a door must be placed across the Vault's entrance. There must also be a door terminal on the outside of the vault. The vault door has a Toughness of 8 and 4 Wounds. Ductways can never be set up so that they lead into the Vault.

When attempting to open the Vault door, Force Door actions succeed on a result of 11 or higher (instead of 9), and Access Terminal actions apply a -4 modifier to the Intelligence check rather than -2.

If a fighter ends an action within 2" of the Glowing Fungus, roll a D6. If the result is higher than their Toughness, or is a natural 6, the fighter succumbs to the toxic spores – make an Injury roll for them (regardless of their Wounds characteristic). If a fighter has an item of wargear that protects them against Gas attacks (such as a respirator or filter plugs), it can also be used against the fungus spores.

Additionally, in scenarios using the Sentries special rules, attackers who are within 2" of Glowing Fungus are easier to see. Add 1 to the result of the dice to see whether they are spotted by a sentry.

WASTE COMPACTOR

Though nothing is ever truly disposed of within the hives of Necromunda, unwanted waste is often compacted for later recycling. The mechanisms by which such waste is disposed of are often used by underhive gangs as a means of torturing or executing captured rivals, and are especially useful in disposing of their corpses afterwards.

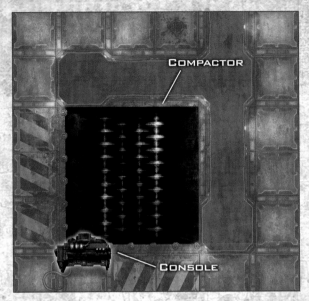

COMPACTOR

CONSOLE

The Compactor is treated as a Pitfall; however, if a model falls into it, they are not taken Out of Action – they are placed within the Compactor, as close as possible to the point from which they fell, and Pinned. Fighters in the Compactor do not have line of sight to fighters outside it unless they are within 1" of the edge, and vice versa.

An Active fighter in the Compactor can make a Basic action to climb out; move them out of the Compactor, placing them as close as possible to it – they are Pinned (there is no need to check whether they fall back in).

Active fighters within 1" of the Console (and not within the Compactor!) can make the following action:

CYCLE WASTE COMPACTOR (BASIC) – Make an Intelligence check for the fighter. If it is passed, any fighters in the Compactor are taken Out of Action. In a campaign battle, no Lasting Injury roll is made; this automatically counts as a 61-65 (Critical Injury).

XENOS NESTING CHAMBER

Whether due to the intentional introduction of off-world fauna or the mutation of native lifeforms, the underhives of Necromunda are host to all manner of strange and often lethal strains, many of which lay their eggs in the deepest, darkest corners they can find. Such locations are extremely perilous to the unwary intruder, as quite apart from the biological hazards of contact with alien spores, whatever it was that laid them might return at any time...

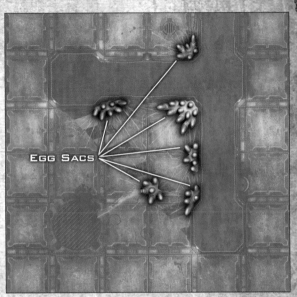

EGG SACS

If a fighter ends an action within 1" of an Egg Sac, roll a D6. On a 1-3, they are attacked by xenos hatchlings – they are Pinned, and suffer D6 Strength 1 hits.

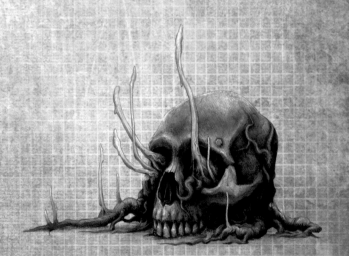

UNDERHIVE ARMOURY

This section contains rules for all of the weapons, armour and wargear available in Necromunda, including items found in the Trading Post chapter of *Gang War,* and the House equipment lists, including those found in *Necromunda: Underhive*. It also contains an up-to-date list of Weapon Traits.

The lists presented so far provide rules for all of the weapons that come with the models released to date. As more gangs and characters are released, rules for any new weapons available to them will be added to the summary and Rare Trade list in future supplements.

PISTOLS

Weapon	Rng S	Rng L	Acc S	Acc L	S	AP	D	Am	Traits
Autopistol	4"	12"	+1	-	3	-	1	4+	Pistol, Rapid Fire (1)
Bolt pistol	6"	12"	+2	-	4	-1	2	6+	Pistol
Hand flamer	-	T	-	-	3	-	1	5+	Blaze, Template
Laspistol	8"	12"	+1	-	3	-	1	2+	Pistol, Plentiful
Plasma pistol – low	6"	12"	+2	-	5	-1	2	5+	Pistol, Scarce
Plasma pistol – maximal	6"	12"	+1	-	7	-2	3	5+	Pistol, Scarce, Unstable
Stub gun	6"	12"	+2	-	3	-	1	4+	Plentiful
– with dumdum rounds	5"	10"	+1	-	4	-	1	4+	Limited

BASIC WEAPONS

Weapon	Rng S	Rng L	Acc S	Acc L	S	AP	D	Am	Traits
Autogun	8"	24"	+1	-	3	-	1	4+	Rapid Fire (1)
Boltgun	12"	24"	+1	-	4	-1	2	6+	Rapid Fire (1)
Combat shotgun – salvo	4"	12"	+1	-	4	-	2	4+	Knockback, Rapid Fire (1)
Combat shotgun – shredder	-	T	-	-	2	-	1	4+	Scattershot, Template
Combat shotgun – firestorm	-	T	-	-	5	-1	1	6+	Blaze, Limited, Template
Lasgun	18"	24"	+1	-	3	-	1	2+	Plentiful
Sawn-off shotgun	4"	8"	+2	-	3	-	1	6+	Plentiful, Scattershot
Shotgun – solid	8"	16"	+1	-	4	-	2	4+	Knockback
Shotgun – scatter	4"	8"	+2	-	2	-	1	4+	Scattershot
Shotgun – executioner	4"	16"	-1	+1	4	-2	2	6+	Knockback, Limited
Shotgun – inferno	4"	16"	+1	-	3	-	1	5+	Blaze, Limited
Stub canon	9"	18"	-	-	5	-	1	3+	Knockback

GRENADES

Weapon	Rng S	Rng L	Acc S	Acc L	S	AP	D	Am	Traits
Blasting charges	-	Sx2	-	-	5	-1	2	5+	Blast (5"), Grenade, Knockback
Choke gas grenade	-	Sx3	-	-	-	-	-	5+	Blast (3"), Gas, Grenade
Frag grenade	-	Sx3	-	-	3	-	1	4+	Blast (3"), Grenade, Knockback
Krak grenade	-	Sx3	-	-1	6	-2	2	4+	Demolitions, Grenade
Photon flash flare	-	Sx3	-	-	-	-	-	5+	Blast (5"), Flash, Grenade
Scare gas grenade	-	Sx3	-	-	-	-	-	6+	Blast (3"), Fear, Gas, Grenade
Smoke bomb	-	Sx3	-	-	-	-	-	4+	Grenade, Smoke

SPECIAL WEAPONS

Weapon	Rng S	L	Acc S	L	S	AP	D	Am	Traits
Flamer	-	T	-	-	4	-1	1	5+	Blaze, Template
Grenade launcher									
– frag grenade	6"	24"	-1	-	3	-	1	6+	Blast (3"), Knockback
– krak grenade	6"	24"	-1	-	6	-2	2	6+	-
– choke gas grenade	6"	24"	-1	-	-	-	-	5+	Blast (3"), Gas, Limited
– scare gas grenade	6"	24"	-1	-	-	-	-	6+	Blast (3"), Fear, Gas, Limited
– smoke grenade	6"	24"	-1	-	-	-	-	4+	Smoke
Meltagun	6"	12"	+1	-	8	-4	3	4+	Melta, Scarce
Needle rifle	9"	18"	-	-	5	-1	1	6+	Scarce, Toxin
'Nightshade' chem-thrower	-	T	-	-	-	-	-	5+	Gas, Template
Plasma gun – low	12"	24"	+2	-	5	-1	2	5+	Rapid Fire (1), Scarce
Plasma gun – maximal	12"	24"	+1	-	7	-2	3	5+	Scarce, Unstable

HEAVY WEAPONS

Weapon	Rng S	L	Acc S	L	S	AP	D	Am	Traits
Harpoon launcher	6"	18"	+2	-	5	-3	1	5+	Drag, Impale, Scarce
Heavy flamer	-	T	-	-	5	-2	1	5+	Blaze, Template
Heavy stubber	20"	40"	-	-1	4	-1	1	4+	Rapid Fire (2), Unwieldy
'Krumper' rivet cannon									
– rapid fire	3"	9"	+2	-	4	-1	2	3+	Rapid Fire (1), Unwieldy
– super-heated	3"	9"	+2	-	6	-2	2	3+	Blaze, Unwieldy
Multi-melta	12"	24"	+1	-	8	-4	3	4+	Blast (3"), Melta, Unwieldy
Plasma cannon – low	18"	36"	+1	-	6	-1	2	5+	Rapid Fire (1), Scarce, Unwieldy
Plasma cannon – maximal	18"	36"	+1	-	8	-2	3	5+	Blast (3"), Scarce, Unwieldy

CLOSE COMBAT WEAPONS

Weapon	Rng S	L	Acc S	L	S	AP	D	Am	Traits
Axe	-	E	-	-	+1	-	1	-	Disarm, Melee
Chainsword	-	E	-	+1	S	-1	1	-	Melee, Parry, Rending
Fighting knife	-	E	-	-	S	-1	1	-	Backstab, Melee
Flail	-	E	-	+1	+1	-	1	-	Entangle, Melee
Maul	-	E	-	-	S	-	2	-	Melee
Power axe	-	E	-	-	+2	-2	1	-	Disarm, Melee, Power
Power hammer	-	E	-	-	+1	-1	2	-	Melee, Power
Power knife	-	E	-	-	+1	-2	1	-	Backstab, Melee, Power
Power sword	-	E	-	-	+1	-2	1	-	Melee, Parry, Power
'Renderizer' serrated axe	-	E	-	-	+2	-1	2	-	Melee, Pulverise, Unwieldy
Servo-claw	-	E	-	-	+2	-	2	-	Melee
Shock whip	-	E	-	-	+1	-	1	-	Melee, Shock
Stiletto knife	-	E	-	+1	S	-	1	-	Melee, Toxin
Stiletto sword	-	E	-	-	S	-1	1	-	Melee, Parry, Toxin
Sword	-	E	-	+1	S	-1	1	-	Melee, Parry
Two-handed axe	-	E	-	-1	+2	-	2	-	Melee, Unwieldy
Two-handed hammer	-	E	-	-1	+1	-	3	-	Knockback, Melee, Unwieldy

KROTOS HARK, BOUNTY HUNTER

220 CREDITS

M	WS	BS	S	T	W	I	A	Ld	Cl	Wil	Int
4"	3+	4+	3	4	2	4+	2	7+	4+	7+	4+

Weapon	Rng S	Rng L	Acc S	Acc L	Str	Ap	D	Am	Traits
Stub cannon	9"	18"	-	-	5	-	1	3+	Knockback
Fighting knife	-	E	-	-	S	-1	1	-	Backstab, Melee

SKILLS: Headbutt, Inspirational, Munitioneer

WARGEAR: Armoured undersuit, furnace plates

KROTOS HARK, GOLIATH BOUNTY HUNTER

Not all Goliaths emerge from the flesh vats disciplined and subservient. Once in a thousand cycles, something goes awry and an aberration is born. Usually these failed gestations are quickly purged, but sometimes the mutation is more subtle. Krotos Hark was born with that most dangerous of gifts; intelligence. He was clever enough to hide his keen mind, and managed to survive long enough to make his way into one of the House gangs. Rather than fight his way up to leadership, something he could certainly have done, he set his sights on a grander destiny.

Hark is a skilled armourer, and valued among gangs for his ability to improve the weapons and gear of those willing to pay. His own furnace plate armour has been hardened against all manner of weapons, while his mask not only hides his identity from his former masters, but can turn aside rounds. Though Hark remains tight-lipped about his ultimate ambitions, it has not gone unnoticed that he seems to be gathering allies and contacts every time he works a contract or fills a bounty. He also seems to take a special interest in jobs that oppose House Goliath. All of this makes some speculate that perhaps Hark is looking to make a permanent change of management among his old bosses.

ARMOUR

A fighter can only be equipped with one kind of armour at a time.

FLAK ARMOUR

Flak armour is made from high-tensile padded fabric, often in the form of a sleeveless jacket which covers the upper torso or armoured pads strapped to the limbs. It offers some protection against low powered weapons and is most useful against blasts and explosive impacts from near-misses.

Flak armour grants a 6+ save roll. Against weapons that use a Blast marker, this is increased to a 5+ save roll.

FURNACE PLATES

Goliath gangers frequently enter battle wearing additional armour that was originally intended to shield the workers stoking the House's roaring plasma furnaces, but which provides excellent protection from enemy weapons.

Furnace plates grant a 6+ save roll. This is increased to a 5+ save roll against attacks made by fighters who are within the fighter's vision arc (the 90° arc to their front); check this before the target is Pinned. If it is not clear whether the attacker is within the target's front arc, use a Vision Arc template to check – if the centre of the attacker's base is within the arc, use the 5+ save roll. Against attacks with the Blast trait, use the centre of the Blast marker in place of the attacker. If the target does not have a facing (for example, if they are Prone), use the 6+ save roll.

MESH ARMOUR

Woven from bonded thermoplas and used either by itself or as the lining of another garment, mesh armour hardens upon impact, absorbing both physical and energy attacks by spreading their force across a wide area.

Mesh armour grants a 5+ save roll.

WARGEAR
AMMO CACHE

Ammo caches are added to the gang's Stash, instead of being carried by a particular fighter. Immediately after the last of the fighters in the crew is set up at the start of a battle, the controlling player can choose to set up any ammo caches from their Stash. If the scenario has an attacker and a defender, and this gang is defending, roll a D6 for each of their ammo caches. On a 1-4, they were not expecting the attackers and the caches cannot be used. On a 5 or 6, they are lucky enough to have them to hand.

Each ammo cache must be set up within 1" of one of their fighters, and within their deployment zone if the scenario has one. It is then deleted from the gang's Stash. During the battle, ammo caches follow the rules on page 66 of the *Necromunda: Underhive* rulebook.

ARMOURED UNDERSUIT

If a fighter is wearing an armoured undersuit, their save roll is improved by 1. For example, if they are wearing flak armour and an armoured undersuit, they would have a 5+ save which would be increased to a 4+ save against blasts. If a fighter does not already have a save roll, an armoured undersuit grants a save of 6+.

BIO-BOOSTER

The first time in each game that an Injury roll is made for a fighter with a bio-booster, one less Injury dice is rolled. If only one dice was being rolled, two dice are rolled and the player controlling the fighter with the bio-booster can discard one of them.

BIO-SCANNER

If a fighter with a bio-scanner is a sentry in a scenario that uses the Sentries special rule, they can attempt to spot attackers even if they are not within their vision arc. In addition, the D6 roll to see whether a fighter is spotted has a +1 modifier (a natural 1 still fails).

CHEM-SYNTH

An Active or Engaged fighter with a chem-synth can make the following action:

Synthesise Poison (Basic) – If the fighter is Engaged, make a Cool check. If the check is passed, or if the fighter is not Engaged, any Gas or Toxin weapons they use until the end of their activation are enhanced and the target's Toughness is reduced by 1 when resolving those attacks.

GOR HALF-HORN, BOUNTY HUNTER

235 CREDITS

M	WS	BS	S	T	W	I	A	Ld	Cl	Wil	Int
4"	3+	4+	4	4	2	4+	1	5+	6+	6+	6+

Weapon	Rng S	Rng L	Acc S	Acc L	Str	Ap	D	Am	Traits
Chainsword	-	E	-	+1	S	-1	1	-	Melee, Parry
Plasma pistol (low)	6"	12"	+2	-	5	-1	2	5+	Pistol, Scarce
Plasma pistol (max)	6"	12"	+1	-	7	-2	3	5+	Pistol, Scarce, Unstable
Shotgun (solid)	8"	16"	+1	-	4	-	2	4+	Knockback
Shotgun (scatter)	4"	8"	+2	-	2	-	1	4+	Scattershot

SKILLS: Berserker, Bull Charge, Fearsome
WARGEAR: Flak armour

GOR HALF-HORN, BEASTMAN BOUNTY HUNTER

Gor Half-horn is a Beastman – a mutant of the strain Homo Sapiens Variatus – and as such is possessed of horribly animalistic features and an unpredictable and violent temperament. These characteristics serve to make Gor a figure of dread in the underhive, but equally, they make him a target for every raving zealot he encounters. As a sanctioned Bounty Hunter, Gor is entitled, in theory at least, to go wherever he will in pursuit of his targets; in reality, he has often found himself the quarry, though so far none have bested him.

Because it is so rare for a Beastman to be sanctioned as a Bounty Hunter, Gor has become the subject of numerous legends throughout the underhive. Some say he was once a member of an Abhuman Auxilia attached to an Astra Militarum regiment, and the sole survivor of a battle of apocalyptic proportions. Others whisper that he was once in the employ of an Inquisitor, whose service he fled for a life among the damned. Some have even claimed that he was not born an Abhuman at all, but a noble scion who developed hideous mutations in his adolescence and fled downhive lest he be put to death by his own kin. None dares to enquire of Gor himself what the truth might be, for all know his response would be swift and fatal.

34

DROP RIG

An Active fighter with a drop rig can make the following action while they are within 1" of the edge of a platform:

DESCEND (BASIC) – The fighter makes a move of up to 3" horizontally and up to 12" vertically. Any vertical movement must be downwards, i.e., towards the ground.

FILTER PLUGS

If a fighter with filter plugs is hit by a weapon with the Gas trait, their Toughness is increased by 1 for the purposes of the roll to see whether they are affected. Filter plugs are one use; if a fighter uses them during a battle, they are deleted from their Fighter card when the battle ends.

GRAPNEL LAUNCHER

An Active fighter with a grapnel launcher can make the following action:

GRAPNEL (DOUBLE) – The fighter can move up to 12" in a straight line, in any direction. This move can take them to a different level, as long as they do not move through any terrain.

GRAV-CHUTE

If the fighter falls or jumps down to a lower level, they do not suffer any damage – they simply move down without any rolls being made.

MEDICAE KIT

When a fighter with a medicae kit assists a friendly fighter's Recovery test, roll an extra Injury dice then choose one to discard.

PHOTO-GOGGLES

A fighter with photo-goggles can attack through smoke clouds (see page 39), and is unaffected by low-light conditions. In addition, if they are hit by a Flash weapon, add 1 to the result of the Initiative test to see whether they are Pinned.

RESPIRATOR

When a ganger with a respirator is hit by a weapon with the Gas trait, their Toughness is increased by 2 for the purposes of the roll to see whether they are affected.

SKINBLADE

If the fighter is captured at the end of a battle, they can attempt to escape. If they do, roll a D6. On a result of 1 or 2, they are unsuccessful. On a result of 3 or 4, they escape but are injured in the process – make a Lasting Injury roll for them. On a result of 5 or 6, they escape. A fighter who escapes is no longer captured; however, their skinblade is lost and removed from their Fighter card.

STIMM-SLUG STASH

A fighter with a stimm-slug stash can use it at the start of their turn, when they are chosen to make an action. Immediately discard one Flesh Wound from the fighter's card, if any are present. Until the end of the round, the fighter's Move, Strength and Toughness characteristics are each increased by 2. At the start of the End phase, roll a D6. On a 1 or 2, the stimm overload is too much – roll an Injury dice and apply the result to the fighter.

STRIP KIT

When a fighter with a strip kit makes an Intelligence check to operate a door terminal or bypass the lock on a loot casket, add 2 to the result.

SCRAPJACK KARL
SONS OF IRON
HOUSE ORLOCK

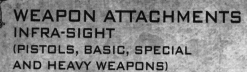

WEAPON ATTACHMENTS
INFRA-SIGHT
(PISTOLS, BASIC, SPECIAL AND HEAVY WEAPONS)

Weapons with the Rapid Fire trait cannot be fitted with an infra-sight. A weapon with an infra-sight can be used to attack through smoke clouds (see page 39), and is unaffected by low-light conditions. In addition, there is no hit modifier when the weapon targets a fighter in partial cover, and a -1 modifier (instead of -2) when it targets a fighter in full cover.

GUNSHROUD
(BASIC WEAPONS AND PISTOLS)

In scenarios that use the Sentries special rules, there is no test to see whether the alarm is raised when a weapon with a gunshroud is fired.

LAS-PROJECTOR
(PISTOLS, BASIC AND SPECIAL WEAPONS)

The weapon's Short Range accuracy bonus is improved by 1 (for example, if it is +1, it becomes +2; if it is -, it becomes +1; if it is -1, it becomes -).

MONO-SIGHT
(BASIC, SPECIAL AND HEAVY WEAPONS)

If the fighter attacks with this weapon after making an Aim action, add 2 to the result of the hit roll instead of 1.

SUSPENSOR
(HEAVY WEAPONS)

A weapon with a suspensor loses the Unwieldy trait with regards to the restrictions descibed in that Trait.

TELESCOPIC SIGHT
(PISTOLS, BASIC AND SPECIAL WEAPONS)

If a fighter attacks with this weapon after making an Aim action, the weapon's Short Range accuracy modifier is used even if the target is within the weapon's Long Range.

WEAPON TRAITS
BACKSTAB

If the attacker is not within the target's vision arc, add 1 to the attack's Strength.

BLAST (3"/5")

The weapon utilises a Blast marker, as described in the *Necromunda: Underhive* rulebook.

BLAZE

After an attack with the Blaze trait has been resolved, roll a D6 if the target was hit but not taken Out of Action. On a 4, 5 or 6 they catch fire – place a Blaze marker on their Fighter card. When a fighter with a Blaze marker is activated, roll a D6, adding 1 to the result for each other Active friendly fighter within 1". On a 6 or more, the flames go out, the Blaze marker is removed and they can act as normal. Otherwise they suffer an immediate Strength 3, AP -1, Damage 1 hit; if they are standing, they move 2D6" in a random direction (determined using the Scatter dice, and stopping if they would move within 1" of an enemy), and their action ends.

A fighter with a Blaze marker can never make any other actions, and cannot make attacks in any way (including Reaction attacks). Alternatively, when an Active or Pinned fighter is activated, they can make a Double action and become Pinned (if they are not already) to add 4 to the result of the roll to see whether the flames go out.

COMBI

A combi-weapon has two profiles. When it is fired, pick one of the two profiles and use it for the attack. Due to the compact nature of the weapons, they often have less capacity for ammunition, and are prone to jamming and other minor issues. When making an Ammo check for either of the weapons, roll twice and apply the worst result. However, unlike most weapons that have two profiles, ammo for the two parts of the combi-weapon are tracked separately – if one profile runs Out of Ammo, the other can still fire unless it has also run Out of Ammo.

DEMOLITIONS

Grenades with the Demolitions trait can be used when making close combat attacks against scenery targets (such as locked doors or scenario objectives). A fighter who uses a grenade in this way makes one attack (regardless of how many Attack dice they would normally roll), which hits automatically.

DISARM

If the hit roll for an attack made with a Disarm weapon is a natural 6, the target cannot use any weapons when making Reaction attacks during that combat – they make unarmed attacks instead.

DRAG

If a fighter is hit by a Drag weapon but not taken Out of Action, the attacker can attempt to drag the target closer after the attack has been resolved. If they do, roll a D6. If the score is equal to or higher than the target's Strength, the target is dragged D3" straight towards the attacker, stopping if they hit any terrain. If they move into another fighter (other than the attacker), both fighters are moved the remaining distance towards the attacker.

If the weapon also has the Impale special rule and hits more than one fighter, only the last fighter to be hit can be dragged.

ENTANGLE

Hits scored by weapons with the Entangle trait cannot be negated by the Parry trait. In addition, if the hit roll for an Entangle weapon is a natural 6, any reaction attacks made by the target have an additional -2 hit modifier.

FEAR

Instead of making an Injury roll for an attack with the Fear trait, the opposing player makes a Nerve test for the target, subtracting 2 from the result. If the test fails, the target is immediately Broken and runs for cover.

FLASH

If a fighter is hit by a Flash weapon, no wound roll is made. Instead, make an Initiative check for the target. If it is failed, they are blinded. A blinded fighter loses their Ready marker; if they do not have a Ready marker, they do not gain a Ready marker at the start of the following round. Until the next time the fighter is activated, they cannot make any attacks other than Reaction attacks, for which any hit rolls will only succeed on a natural 6.

GAS

When a fighter is hit by an attack made by a Gas weapon, they are not Pinned and a wound roll is not made. Instead, roll a D6. If the result is equal to or higher than the target's Toughness, or is a natural 6, make an Injury roll for them (regardless of their Wounds characteristic) – no save roll can be made.

GRENADE

The weapon uses the Grenade rules, as described in the *Necromunda: Underhive* rulebook.

IMPALE

If an attack made by this weapon hits and wounds the target, and the save roll is unsuccessful (or no save roll is made), the projectile continues through them and might hit another fighter! Trace a straight line from the target, directly away from the attacker. If there are any fighters within 1" of this line, and within the weapon's Long Range, the one that is closest to the target is at risk of being hit. Roll a D6 – on a 3 or more, resolve the weapon's attack against that fighter, subtracting 1 from the Strength. The projectile can continue through multiple fighters in this way, but if the Strength is reduced to 0, it cannot hit any more fighters.

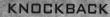

KNOCKBACK

If the hit roll for a weapon with the Knockback trait is equal to or higher than the target's Strength (before any modifiers are applied), they are immediately moved 1" directly away from the attacking fighter. If the fighter cannot be moved the full 1" because of a wall, obstacle or another fighter, they move as far as possible and the attack's Damage is increased by 1.

If a Blast weapon has the Knockback trait, roll a D6 for each fighter that is hit. If the result is equal to or higher than their Strength, they are Knocked Back as described above – however, they are moved directly away from the centre of the Blast marker instead. If the centre of the Blast marker was over the centre of their base, roll a Scatter dice to determine which way they are moved (re-rolling hits).

If a Melee weapon has the Knockback trait, the attacking fighter can choose to follow the target up, moving directly towards them after they have been Knocked Back to remain in base contact. If the attack was made across a barricade, the attacker cannot do this.

LIMITED

This special rule is applied to some special ammo types which can be purchased for weapons. If a weapon fails an Ammo check while using Limited ammo, they have run out – that ammo type is deleted from their Fighter card, and cannot be used again until more of that special ammo is purchased from the Trading Post. This is in addition to the normal rules for the weapon running Out of Ammo. The weapon can still be reloaded as normal, using its remaining profile(s).

MELEE

This weapon can be used during close combat attacks.

MELTA

If this weapon is fired at Short Range, no Injury roll is made – instead, the target automatically goes Out of Action.

PARRY

After an enemy makes close combat attacks against a fighter armed with a Parry weapon, the fighter can force the attacking player to re-roll one successful hit. If the fighter is armed with two Parry weapons, they can force the attacking player to re-roll two successful hits instead.

PISTOL

Pistols can be used to make ranged attacks, and can also be used in close combat as described in the *Necromunda: Underhive* rulebook. Note that their Accuracy bonus only applies when shooting.

PLENTIFUL

Ammunition for this weapon is incredibly common. When reloading it, no Ammo check is required – it is automatically reloaded.

POWER

The weapon is surrounded by a crackling power field. Attacks made by Power weapons cannot be parried except by other Power weapons. In addition, if the hit roll for a Power weapon is a 6, no save roll can be made against the attack and its Damage is increased by 1.

PULVERISE

After making an Injury roll for an attack made by this weapon, the attacking player can roll a D6. If the result is equal to or higher than the target's Toughness, or is a natural 6, they can change one Injury dice from a Flesh Wound result to a Serious Injury result.

RAPID FIRE (X)

When firing with a Rapid Fire weapon, a successful hit roll scores a number of hits equal to the number of bullet holes on the Firepower dice. In addition, the controlling player can roll more than one Firepower dice, up to the number shown in brackets (for example, when firing a Rapid Fire (2) weapon, up to two Firepower dice can be rolled). Make an Ammo check for each Ammo symbol that is rolled. If any of them fail, the gun runs Out of Ammo. If two or more of them fail, the gun has jammed and cannot be used for the rest of the battle.

If a Rapid Fire weapon scores more than one hit, the hits can be split between multiple targets. The first must be allocated to the original target, but the remainder can be allocated to other fighters within 3" of the first who are also within range and line of sight. These must not be any harder to hit than the original target – if a target in the open is hit, an obscured target cannot have hits allocated to it. Allocate all of the hits before making any wound rolls.

SCARCE

Ammunition is hard to come by for Scarce weapons, and as such they cannot be reloaded – once they run Out of Ammo, they cannot be used again during the battle.

SCATTERSHOT

When a target is hit by a scattershot attack, make D6 wound rolls instead of 1.

SHOCK

If the hit roll for a Shock weapon is a natural 6, the wound roll is considered to automatically succeed (no wound roll needs to be made).

SMOKE

Smoke weapons do not cause hits on fighters – they do not cause Pinning, and cannot inflict wounds. Instead, mark the location where they hit with a counter. They generate an area of dense smoke, which extends 2.5" out from the centre of the counter; a 5" Blast marker can be used to determine this area, but it should be considered to extend vertically as well as horizontally. Fighters can move through the smoke, but it blocks line of sight, so attacks cannot be made into, out of or through it. In the End phase, roll a D6; on a 4 or less, the cloud dissipates and the counter is removed.

TEMPLATE

Template weapons use the Flame template to determine how many targets they hit, as described in the *Necromunda: Underhive* rulebook.

TOXIN

Instead of making an Injury roll for a toxin attack, roll 2D6. The target's controlling player rolls a D6 and adds the target's Toughness. If the target's roll is higher, they shrug off the toxin's effects. If the rolls are equal, the target is Seriously Injured. If the 2D6 roll is higher, the target goes Out of Action.

VERSATILE

If the wielder of a Versatile weapon is Engaged, it counts as a Melee weapon. Otherwise, it counts as a Ranged weapon.

UNSTABLE

If the Ammo symbol is rolled on the Firepower dice when attacking with this weapon, there is a chance the weapon will overheat in addition to needing an Ammo check. Roll a D6. On a 1, 2 or 3, the weapon suffers a catastrophic overload and the attacker is taken Out of Action. The attack is still resolved against the target.

UNWIELDY

A Shoot action made with this weapon counts as a Double action as opposed to a Single action. In addition, a fighter who uses an Unwieldy melee weapon in close combat cannot use a second weapon at the same time – this one requires both hands to use.

HANDSOME DRAK
SUMP DOGS
HOUSE ORLOCK

THE DESERTER,
HUMAN BOUNTY HUNTER

No one knows the real name of the Deserter, only that by his tattoos he once served in the legendary Necromundan 8th. The crazy old soldier lives downhive in a booby-trapped warren, with every approach a deadly killing ground. Leaders often need to send at least a few Juves when contracting the Deserter, as he can be a little trigger happy when it comes to those who knock on his door. The skills he brings to a fight, however, are always worth it, and there are few individuals as talented when it comes to laying traps or setting ambushes.

Why the authorities tolerate the Deserter is a mystery to underhive gangs. Some believe he was a disgraced general that lost his entire regiment in some off-world war, and was given the choice of execution or exile to hive bottom. Others reckon he was a war hero, grievously wounded (as his skull plate seems to attest), who wandered down from the spire after losing his memory. Then there are those who say he is called the Deserter because that is just what he is, and Helmawr's cronies simply stopped trying to bring him in after their enforcers kept failing to come back. Whatever the truth, the Deserter is a cantankerous old fighter that gang fighters underestimate at their peril!

THE DESERTER, BOUNTY HUNTER

225 CREDITS

M	WS	BS	S	T	W	I	A		Ld	Cl	Wil	Int
4"	3+	4+	3	4	2	4+	2		7+	6+	7+	8+

Weapon	Rng S	L	Acc S	L	Str	Ap	D	Am	Traits
Shotgun – solid	8"	16"	+1	-	4	-	2	4+	Knockback
Shotgun – scatter	4"	8"	+2	-	2	-	1	4+	Scattershot
Frag grenades	-	Sx3	-	-	3	-	1	4+	Blast (3"), Grenade, Knockback
Fighting knife	-	E	-	-	S	-1	1	-	Backstab, Melee

SKILLS: Medicae, Mentor, Overseer

WARGEAR: Armoured undersuit, flak armour

SKILLS

This section lists all of the skills that are available to fighters. Each entry in the section lists the skill's name, its set (in parentheses), then its rules.

The following table summarises each of the skill sets, and can be used (by rolling a D6) to determine a random skill from one of the sets.

D6	Agility	Brawn	Combat	Cunning	Ferocity	Leadership	Shooting	Savant
1	Catfall	Bull Charge	Combat Master	Backstab	Berserker	Commanding Presence	Fast Shot	Ballistics Expert
2	Clamber	Bulging Biceps	Counter-attack	Escape Artist	Impetuous	Inspirational	Gunfighter	Connected
3	Dodge	Crushing Blow	Disarm	Evade	Fearsome	Iron Will	Hip Shooting	Fixer
4	Mighty Leap	Headbutt	Parry	Infiltrate	Nerves of Steel	Mentor	Marksman	Medicae
5	Spring Up	Hurl	Step Aside	Lie Low	True Grit	Overseer	Precision Shot	Munitioneer
6	Sprint	Iron Jaw	Rain of Blows	Overwatch	Unstoppable	Regroup	Trick Shot	Savvy Trader

SKILLS

BACKSTAB (CUNNING)
Any close combat weapons used by this fighter gain the Backstab trait. If they already have this Trait, add 2 to the attacker's Strength rather than 1 when the Trait is used.

BALLISTICS EXPERT (SAVANT)
When this fighter makes an Aim action, make an Intelligence check for them. If it passes, they gain an additional +1 modifier to their hit roll.

BERSERKER (FEROCITY)
When this fighter makes close combat attacks as part of a Charge action, they roll an additional Attack dice.

BULL CHARGE (BRAWN)
When the fighter makes close combat attacks as part of a Charge action, any Melee weapons they use gain the Knockback trait and are resolved at +1 Strength.

BULGING BICEPS (BRAWN)
If any weapons carried by the fighter have the Unwieldy trait, the effects of Unwieldy are ignored.

CATFALL (AGILITY)
When this fighter falls or jumps down from a ledge, they count as having moved half the vertical distance. In addition, if they are not Seriously Injured or taken Out of Action by a fall, make an Initiative test for them – if it is passed, they remain standing rather than being Pinned.

CLAMBER (AGILITY)
When the fighter climbs, the vertical distance they move is not halved. In other words, they always count as climbing up or down a ladder.

COMBAT MASTER (COMBAT)
The fighter never suffers penalties to their hit rolls for interference, and can always grant assists regardless of how many enemy fighters they are engaged with.

COMMANDING PRESENCE (LEADERSHIP)
If a group is activated, and this fighter is chosen to lead the group, it can include one more fighter than normal (i.e., a Champion could activate two other fighters instead of one, or a Leader could activate three).

CONNECTED (SAVANT)
This fighter can make a Trade action in the post-battle sequence in addition to any other actions they make (meaning they could even make two Trade actions). They cannot do this if they are not able to make any actions.

COUNTER-ATTACK (COMBAT)
When this fighter makes Reaction attacks in close combat, they roll one additional Attack dice for each of the attacker's attacks that failed to hit (whether they missed, they were parried, etc).

CRUSHING BLOW (BRAWN)

Before rolling to hit for the fighter's close combat attacks, the controlling player can nominate one dice to make a Crushing Blow. This cannot be a dice that is rolling to hit for a pistol. If that dice hits, the attack's Strength and Damage are each increased by 1.

DISARM (COMBAT)

Any Melee weapons used by the fighter gain the Disarm trait. If a weapon already has this Trait then the target will be disarmed on a natural roll of a 5 or 6, not just a 6.

DODGE (AGILITY)

If this fighter suffers a wound from a ranged attack or close combat attack, roll a D6. On a 6, the attack is dodged and has no effect; otherwise, continue to make a save roll as normal.

If the model dodges a weapon that uses a Blast marker or Flame template, a roll of 6 does not automatically cancel the attack – instead, it allows the fighter to move up to 2" before seeing whether they are hit. They cannot move within 1" of an enemy fighter.

ESCAPE ARTIST (CUNNING)

When this fighter makes a Retreat action, add 2 to the result of the Initiative check (a natural 1 still fails). In addition, if this fighter is Captured at the end of a battle, roll a D6. On a result of 2 or more, they slip away and are not Captured.

EVADE (CUNNING)

If an enemy targets this fighter with a ranged attack, and this fighter is Active and not in partial cover or full cover, there is an additional -1 modifier to the hit roll, or a -2 modifier if they are at Long Range.

FAST SHOT (SHOOTING)

This fighter treats the Shoot action as Simple rather than Basic as long as they do not attack with an Unwieldy weapon for either action.

FEARSOME (FEROCITY)

If an enemy makes a Charge action that targets this fighter, they must make a Willpower check before moving. If the check is failed, they cannot move and their action ends immediately.

OLD JON GREYSON
ASH RUNNERS
HOUSE ORLOCK

FIXER (SAVANT)

In the Gain Rewards step of the post-battle sequence, as long as this fighter is not Captured or In Recovery, their gang earns an additional D3x10 credits. Note that they do not need to have taken part in the battle.

GUNFIGHTER (SHOOTING)

If the fighter attacks with two pistols (see page 58 of the *Necromunda: Underhive* rulebook), they do not suffer the -1 penalty to the hit rolls and can, if they wish, target a different enemy with each pistol.

HEADBUTT (BRAWN)

If the fighter is Engaged, they can make the following action:

HEADBUTT (BASIC) – Pick an Engaged enemy fighter and roll two D6. If either result is equal to or higher than their Toughness, they suffer a hit with a Strength equal to this fighter's Strength +2, resolved at Damage 2. However, if both dice score lower than the enemy fighter's Toughness, this fighter instead suffers a hit equal to their own Strength.

HIP SHOOTING (SHOOTING)

If the fighter is Active, they can make the following action:

RUN AND GUN (DOUBLE) – The fighter makes a Double Move then makes an attack with a Ranged weapon. The hit roll has an additional -1 modifier, and Unwieldy weapons cannot be used.

YAR UMBRA, VOID-BORN BOUNTY HUNTER

Vast quantities of off-world trade comes to Necromunda via the Eye of Selene. Carrying these cargoes are all manner of ships, their crews often made up of void-born spacers who spend their lives traversing the inky galactic wilds. Yar Umbra came to Hive Primus on the chartist vessel the *Halcyon Dawn*. Unfortunately for Yar, when his ship left he was not on it, for he was intentionally marooned by the deck master for some unknown infraction, which, some say, was centred around what it is that he hides beneath his hood.

Embittered by his abandonment, Yar yearns to return to the stars, and has turned his talents to claiming bounties, in the hopes of one day obtaining passage on a vessel and hunting down the *Halcyon Dawn*. In the interim, Yar has found that though he despises his planet-bound existence, he is very much at home in the confined tunnels of Necromunda. The stinking depths of a hive are much the same as those of a void ship (if even a bit more forgiving), and equipped with enviro-fliters and gas-plugs, Yar is well-protected from local hazards. Darkness is also an environment Yar knows well, and with his custom maw-pattern longlas even a flicker of movement is enough for the void-born sniper to bring down his prey.

YAR UMBRA, BOUNTY HUNTER

220 CREDITS

M	WS	BS	S	T	W	I	A	Ld	Cl	Wil	Int
4"	4+	2+	3	4	2	3+	1	7+	5+	7+	7+

Weapon	Rng S	Rng L	Acc S	Acc L	Str	Ap	D	Am	Traits
Lasgun	18"	24"	+1	-	3	-	1	2+	Plentiful, Telescopic sight
Fighting knife	-	E	-	-	S	-1	1	-	Backstab, Melee

SKILLS: Infiltrate, Marksman, Overwatch

WARGEAR: Flak armour, photo-googles, respirator

HURL (BRAWN)

If the fighter is Active or Engaged, they can make the following action:

THROW OPPONENT (BASIC) – Pick an engaged enemy fighter or a Seriously Injured enemy fighter in base contact. If that fighter is standing, the opposing player can make an Initiative check for them; if this is failed, or if the fighter was Seriously Injured, the enemy fighter is hurled. Pick a direction, then move the enemy fighter D3" in that direction – if they were standing, they are Pinned after moving. If they hit a standing fighter or piece of terrain (other than a low obstruction), they stop moving and suffer a Strength 3 hit. If they hit another fighter, that fighter also suffers a Strength 3 hit and is Pinned.

IMPETUOUS (FEROCITY)

When this fighter Consolidates at the end of a close combat, they can move up to 4" instead of up to 2".

JO CHANCE
SUMP DOGS
HOUSE ORLOCK

INFILTRATE (CUNNING)

If this fighter should be set up at the start of a battle, they are instead placed to one side. Then, immediately before the start of the first round, their controlling player sets them up anywhere on the battlefield that is not visible to any enemy fighters, and not within 6" of any of them. If both players have fighters with this skill, take turns to set one up, starting with the winner of a roll-off.

INSPIRATIONAL (LEADERSHIP)

If a friendly fighter within 6" of this fighter fails a Cool check, make a Leadership check for this fighter. If it passes, the Cool check is also treated as having passed.

IRON JAW (BRAWN)

This fighter's Toughness is treated as being 2 higher than normal when another fighter makes unarmed attacks against them in close combat.

IRON WILL (LEADERSHIP)

Subtract 1 from the result of any Bottle rolls while this fighter is on the battlefield and not Seriously Injured.

LIE LOW (CUNNING)

While this fighter is Prone, enemy fighters cannot target them with ranged attacks unless they are within the attacking weapon's Short Range. Weapons that do not have a Short Range are unaffected by this rule.

MARKSMAN (SHOOTING)

The fighter is not affected by the rules for Target Priority (see page 58 of the *Necromunda: Underhive* rulebook). In addition, if the hit roll for a ranged attack made by the fighter is a natural 6 (when using a weapon that does not have the Blast trait), they score a critical hit and the attack's Damage is doubled (if they are firing a Rapid Fire weapon, only the first hit's Damage is doubled).

MEDICAE (SAVANT)

When this fighter assists a friendly fighter who is making a Recovery test, re-roll any Out of Action results. If the result of a re-rolled dice is also Out of Action, the result stands.

MENTOR (LEADERSHIP)

Make a Leadership check for this fighter each time another fighter within 6" gains a point of Experience. If the check passes, that fighter gains 2 Experience instead of 1.

MIGHTY LEAP (AGILITY)

This fighter can attempt to leap (see page 10 of *Gang War*) across gaps that are no wider than their Movement characteristic. If the gap is wider than half their Movement characteristic, the Initiative test has a -1 modifier.

MUNITIONEER (SAVANT)

Whenever an Ammo check is failed for this fighter, or another fighter from the same gang within 6", it can be re-rolled.

NERVES OF STEEL (FEROCITY)

When the fighter is hit by a ranged attack, make a Cool check for them. If it is passed, they are not Pinned.

OVERSEER (LEADERSHIP)

If the fighter is Active, they can attempt to make the following action:

Order (Double) – Pick a friendly fighter within 12". That fighter can immediately make two actions as though it were their turn, even if they are not Ready. If they are Ready, these actions do not remove their Ready status.

OVERWATCH (CUNNING)

If this fighter is Active and Readied, they can interrupt a visible enemy fighter's action as soon as it is declared but before it is carried out. This fighter loses their Ready marker, then immediately makes a Shoot action, targeting the enemy fighter whose action has been declared. If the enemy is Pinned or Seriously Injured, their turn ends immediately – their action is not made.

PARRY (COMBAT)

The fighter can parry attacks as though they were carrying a weapon with the Parry trait. If they already have one or more weapons with this Trait, they can parry one additional attack.

PRECISION SHOT (SHOOTING)

If the hit roll for a ranged attack made by the fighter is a natural 6 (when using a weapon that does not have the Blast trait), the shot hits an exposed area and the opponent cannot make an armour save.

RAIN OF BLOWS (COMBAT)

This fighter treats the Fight action as Simple rather than Basic.

REGROUP (LEADERSHIP)

If this fighter is Active at the end of their turn, make a Leadership check for them. If it passes, each friendly Broken fighter within 6" recovers from being Broken.

SAVVY TRADER (SAVANT)

When this fighter makes a Trade action in the post-battle sequence, add 1 to the result of the roll to see whether the item is available and reduce the cost of the item by 20 credits (to a minimum of 10).

SPRING UP (AGILITY)

If this fighter is Pinned when they are activated, make an Initiative check for them. If the check is passed, the fighter can make a free Stand Up action.

SPRINT (AGILITY)

If this fighter makes two Move actions in a turn, they can use the second one to Sprint. This lets them make a Double Move instead of a Standard Move for that action.

STEP ASIDE (COMBAT)

If the fighter is hit in close combat, the fighter can attempt to step aside. Make an Initiative check for them. If the check is passed, the attack misses. This skill can only be used once per enemy in each round of close combat – in other words, if an enemy makes more than one attack, the fighter can only attempt to step aside from one of them.

TRICK SHOT (SHOOTING)

When this fighter makes ranged attacks, they do not suffer a penalty to the hit roll for the target being Engaged or in Partial Cover. In addition, if the target is in Full Cover, they suffer a -1 penalty instead of -2.

TRUE GRIT (FEROCITY)

When making an Injury roll for the fighter, roll one less Injury dice (for example, a Damage 2 weapon would roll one dice). Against attacks with Damage 1, roll two dice – the player controlling the fighter with True Grit can then choose to discard one before resolving the dice effects.

UNSTOPPABLE (FEROCITY)

Before making a Recovery check for this fighter in the End phase, roll a D6. On a result of 4 or more, one Flesh Wound they have suffered is discarded. If they do not have any Flesh Wounds and the result is 4 or more, roll one additional dice for their Recovery check.

REFERENCE

This section of *Gang War Two* provides a useful summary of key tables players are most likely to need to refer to during play, as well as a list of page references where the most useful rules may be found.

ADVANCEMENTS (SEE PAGE 16 OF *GANG WAR*)

Cost	Advancement – Leaders, Champions, Juves, Specialists	Value
3 XP	+1 Willpower or Intelligence	+5 credits
4 XP	+1 Leadership or Cool	+10 credits
5 XP	+1 Initiative	+10 credits
5 XP	+1 Movement	+10 credits
6 XP	+1 Weapon Skill or Ballistic Skill	+20 credits
6 XP	Random Primary skill	+20 credits
8 XP	+1 Strength or Toughness	+30 credits
9 XP	Choose Primary skill	+20 credits
9 XP	Random Secondary skill	+35 credits
12 XP	+1 Wounds or Attacks	+45 credits
12 XP	Promote Specialist to Champion, Random Primary skill.	+40 credits
15 XP	Random skill (any set)	+50 credits

2D6	Advancement – Gangers (not including Specialists)	Value
2	The fighter becomes a Specialist.	–
3-4	+1 Weapon Skill or Ballistic Skill	+5 credits
5-6	+1 Strength or Toughness	+30 credits
7	+1 Movement or Initiative	+10 credits
8-9	+1 Willpower or Intelligence	+20 credits
10-11	+1 Leadership or Cool	+10 credits
12	The fighter becomes a Specialist.	–

RANDOM SKILLS

D6	Agility	Brawn	Combat	Cunning	Ferocity	Leadership	Shooting	Savant
1	Catfall	Bull Charge	Combat Master	Backstab	Berserker	Commanding Presence	Fast Shot	Ballistics Expert
2	Clamber	Bulging Biceps	Counter-attack	Escape Artist	Impetuous	Inspirational	Gunfighter	Connected
3	Dodge	Crushing Blow	Disarm	Evade	Fearsome	Iron Will	Hip Shooting	Fixer
4	Mighty Leap	Headbutt	Parry	Infiltrate	Nerves of Steel	Mentor	Marksman	Medicae
5	Spring Up	Hurl	Step Aside	Lie Low	True Grit	Overseer	Precision Shot	Munitioneer
6	Sprint	Iron Jaw	Rain of Blows	Overwatch	Unstoppable	Regroup	Trick Shot	Savvy Trader

SCENARIO TABLE

2D6	Result
2-3	The player with the higher Gang Rating chooses which scenario to play. If both players have the same Gang Rating, the winner of a roll-off chooses which scenario to play. If there is an attacker and a defender, the player who chose the scenario is the attacker.
4-6	Play the Stand-off scenario (see page page 55 of *Gang War*).
7-12	The player with the lower Gang Rating chooses which scenario to play. If both players have the same Gang Rating, the winner of a roll-off chooses which scenario to play. If there is an attacker and a defender, the player who chose the scenario is the attacker.

FALLING AND JUMPING DOWN
(SEE PAGES 9-10 OF *GANG WAR*)

Distance	Jumping Down Modifier	Falling Strength	AP	Damage
1"-2"	-	-	-	-
3"-5"	-1	3	-	1
6"-8"	-2	5	-1	1
7"-9"	-3	7	-2	2
10"+	-4	9	-3	3

LASTING INJURIES (SEE PAGE 18 OF *GANG WAR*)

D66	Lasting Injury
11	**Lesson Learned.** Into recovery, +D3 Experience.
12-26	**Out Cold.** No effect.
31-45	**Grievous Injury.** Into recovery.
46	**Humiliated.** Into recovery, -1 Leadership and Cool.
51	**Head Injury.** Into recovery, -1 Intelligence and Willpower.
52	**Eye Injury.** Into recovery, -1 Ballistic Skill.
53	**Hand Injury.** Into recovery, -1 Weapon Skill.
54	**Hobbled.** Into recovery, -1 Movement.
55	**Spinal Injury.** Into recovery, -1 Strength.
56	**Enfeebled.** Into recovery, -1 Toughness.
61-65	**Critical Injury.** Dead, unless saved by a Doc.
66	**Memorable Death.** Dead – attacker gains +1 Experience.

PRE-BATTLE SEQUENCE
(SEE PAG 20 OF *GANG WAR*)

1. Buy Advancements and Recruit Hired Guns
2. Determine Scenario
3. Set up Battlefield
4. Draw Tactics Cards
5. Choose Crews
6. Deploy

POST-BATTLE SEQUENCE
(SEE PAGE 22 OF *GANG WAR*)

1. Wrap Up
2. Collect Income (first battle of the cycle only)
3. Receive Rewards
4. Post-battle Actions
5. Update Roster
6. Report Results

USEFUL PAGE REFERENCES

Special Territory Table – page 28 of *Gang War*
The Trading Post – page 30 of *Gang War*
Underhive Armoury – page 30
Weapon Traits – page 36
Skills – page 41
Goliath House List – page 45 of *Gang War*
Escher House List – page 49 of *Gang War*
Orlock House List – page 9
Hired Guns – page 13
Hangers-on – page 16

"Ten fingers, two arms, two legs, a pair of eyes and most of your teeth – you have a veritable embarrassment of appendages, just you wait, we'll soon sort that out…"

The Queen of Blades, Omega Bloodmaidens, House Escher

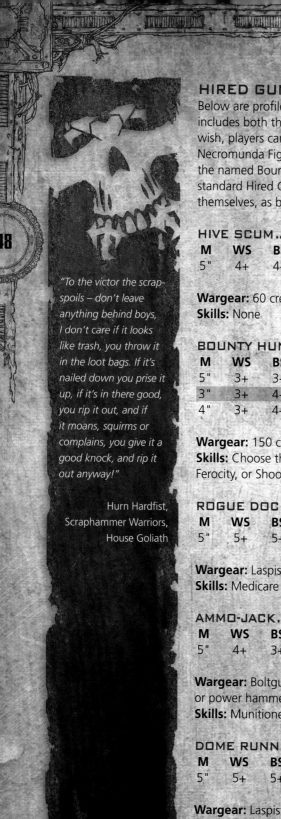

HIRED GUNS PROFILES

Below are profile summaries for the Hired Guns found throughout this book. This includes both the standard Hired Guns and the named Bounty Hunters. If they wish, players can transpose the characteristics, skills, wargear, etc, onto a blank Necromunda Fighter card for quick reference during their games. Note that while the named Bounty Hunters have been designed broadly within the bounds of the standard Hired Guns rules, they include skills, wargear and characteristics unique to themselves, as befits such singularly dangerous individuals!

HIVE SCUM...30 CREDITS

M	WS	BS	S	T	W	I	A	LD	Cl	Wil	Int
5"	4+	4+	3	3	1	4+	1	8+	8+	8+	8+

Wargear: 60 credits worth of equipment; no more than three weapons.
Skills: None

BOUNTY HUNTER...80 CREDITS

M	WS	BS	S	T	W	I	A	Ld	Cl	Wil	Int
5"	3+	3+	3	3	2	3+	1	7+	5+	6+	6+
3"	3+	4+	3	4	2	5+	1	5+	7+	5+	5+
4"	3+	4+	3	4	1	4+	2	7+	6+	7+	8+

Wargear: 150 credits worth of equipment; no more than five weapons.
Skills: Choose three at random from: Agility, Brawn, Combat, Cunning, Ferocity, or Shooting.

ROGUE DOC..50 CREDITS

M	WS	BS	S	T	W	I	A	Ld	Cl	Wil	Int
5"	5+	5+	2	3	1	4+	1	9+	8+	7+	5+

Wargear: Laspistol or stub gun; medicae kit.
Skills: Medicare

AMMO-JACK..50 CREDITS

M	WS	BS	S	T	W	I	A	Ld	Cl	Wil	Int
5"	4+	3+	3	3	1	5+	1	9+	7+	6+	7+

Wargear: Boltgun or combat shotgun with salvo and scatter ammo; power sword or power hammer; mesh armour
Skills: Munitioneer

DOME RUNNER..20 CREDITS

M	WS	BS	S	T	W	I	A	Ld	Cl	Wil	Int
5"	5+	5+	3	3	1	3+	1	10+	9+	7+	8+

Wargear: Laspistol or stub gun; fighting knife or axe
Skills: Lie Low

SLOPPER..20 CREDITS

M	WS	BS	S	T	W	I	A	Ld	Cl	Wil	Int
4"	4+	4+	2	3	1	3+	1	9+	9+	5+	7+

Wargear: Fighting knife
Skills: None